BrightRED Study Guide

CfE HIGHER

ENGLISH

Dr Christopher Nicol

BrightRED
PUBLISHING

First published in 2014 by:
Bright Red Publishing Ltd
1 Torphichen Street
Edinburgh
EH3 8HX

Reprinted with corrections 2015

A CIP record for this book is available from the British Library.

ISBN 978-1-906736-61-3

With thanks to:
PDQ Digital Media Solutions Ltd, Bungay (layout) and Sue Moody, Bright Writing (copy-edit). Cover design and series book design by Caleb Rutherford – e i d e t i c.

Acknowledgements
The author would like to make special thanks to Dr Sandra Percy, Professor Alan Riach and Dr Christine Robinson (Scottish National Dictionaries) for their help with this project.

Every effort has been made to seek all copyright-holders. If any have been overlooked, then Bright Red Publishing will be delighted to make the necessary arrangements.

Permission has been sought from all relevant copyright holders and Bright Red Publishing are grateful for the use of the following:

Garry Knight (CC BY-SA 2.0)[1] (p 6); kate_sept2004/iStock.com (p 6); Extract by Neil Gaiman from 'Why our future depends on libraries, reading and daydreaming' in the Guardian, 15 October 2013. Copyright Guardian News & Media Ltd 2013 (p 8); Fortress Orkney/Orkney Islands Coucil (p 9); Extract by Christopher Nicol, 'Eric Linklater's 'Private Angelo' and 'The Dark of Summer', (ASLS, Glasgow 2012) (p 9 and 11); Extract from 'Happy City: Transforming Our Lives Through Urban Design' by Charles Montgomery (Penguin Press 2013) Copyright © Charles Montgomery, 2013 (pp 10 & 11); Extract from, 'Yes, the floods are awful, but we must keep a sense of proportion', by Peter Oborne in the Daily Telegraph, 12th Feb 2014 © Telegraph Media Group Limited 2014 (p 11); Extract by Sophie Heawood, 'It's not enough to be a celebrity brand. Today you must be a guru.', in the Guardian, 1st January 2014. Copyright Guardian News & Media Ltd 2014 (p 13); Scandic Hotels (CC BY 3.0)[2] (p 13); Extract from, 'Living in Cyburbia', by James Harkin in the Telegraph, 29th January 2011 © Telegraph Media Group Limited 2011 (p 13); Extract from 'Venice' by Jan Morris (Faber & Faber 1993) (pp 15 & 24); Extract from, 'A whole new e-chapter', by by James Harkin in the Guardian, 26th April 2011. Copyright Guardian News & Media Ltd 2011 (pp 15 & 26); An extract and the front cover of 'A Clash of Kings' by George R R Martin (Harper Voyager, 1999) © HarperCollins Publishers (p 20); Tony Hisgett (CC BY 2.0)[3] (p 20); Caleb Rutherford e i d e t i c (p 21); Extract from President Barack Obama's election night victory speech, November 7, 2012 © Whitehouse.gov (CC BY 3.0)[2] (p 23); StockMonkeys.com (CC BY 2.0)[3] (p 25); The front cover of 'Vanity Fair' © Four Corners Books (p 26); Extract abridged from 'Dark lands: the grim truth behind the "Scandinavian miracle"' by Michael Booth, in the Guardian, 27th January 2014. Copyright Guardian News & Media Ltd 2014 (pp 28 – 29); Dennis Jarvis (CC BY-SA 2.0)[1] (p 29); Dennis Jarvis (CC BY-SA 2.0)[1] (p 30); Extract abridged from "Denmark Is Considered The Happiest Country. You'll Never Guess Why.", in the Huffington Post, October 22nd 2013 © PARS International Corp., Inc. (p 30); Jacob Martin (CC BY 2.0)[3] (p 32); briefshots/iStock.com (p 33); Caleb Rutherford e i d e t i c (p 36); Caleb Rutherford e i d e t i c (p 36); Phil Kahlina for Stan Hywet Hall & Gardens © 2008 (p 37); Extracts from 'The Moon Belongs to Everyone: Making Theatre with 7:84' by Elizabeth MacLennan (Methuen 1990) (pp 38 & 39); National Library of Scotland (p 39); Extracts from 'The Cheviot, the Stag and the Black, Black Oil' by John McGrath published by Methuen Drama, an imprint of Bloomsbury Publishing (pp 41 & 43 –47); An illustration from 'The Moon Belongs to Everyone: Making Theatre with 7:84' by Elizabeth MacLennan (Methuen 1990) (p 42); Extract from 'A Good Night Out', by John McGrath (Eyre Methuen: 1981) (p 45); James McNaught (p 50); Book cover for 'The Trick is to Keep Breathing' published by Vintage © The Random House Group Ltd (p 50); Caleb Rutherford e i d e t i c (p 51); jfg/freeimages.com (p 53); Extracts from 'The Trick is to Keep Breathing' by Janice Galloway, published by Vintage © The Random House Group Ltd (p 54-59); aastock/shutterstock.com (p 56); cjaphoto/iStock.com (p 57); Winai_Tepsuttinun/iStock.com (p 59); Freddie Phillips (CC BY 2.0)[3] (p 62); Caleb Rutherford e i d e t i c (p 62); Extract by Don Paterson in Tony Curtis (ed.) 'How poets Work' (Seren 1996) (p 63); A quote from Don Paterson in 'The Literature of Scotland: The Twentieth Century' by Roderick Watson (Palgrave Macmillan 2007) (p 63); Extracts from 'Waking with Russell' by Don Paterson, taken from 'Landing Light' (Faber & Faber 2003). Reproduced by permission of the author c/o Rogers, Coleridge & White Ltd., 20 Powis Mews, London W11 1JN (p 64); Extract from the essay 'The Dilemma of the Poet' by Don Paterson in Tony Curtis (ed.) 'How poets Work', (Seren 1996) (p 64); The poem 'The Thread' by Don Paterson from 'Landing Light' (Faber & Faber 2003). Reproduced by permission of the author c/o Rogers, Coleridge & White Ltd.(p 65); The poem '11.00 Baldovan' by Don Paterson, taken from 'New Scottish Poetry', edited by Gordon Liddell, Anne Gifford (Heinemann 2001) Reproduced by permission of the author c/o Rogers, Coleridge & White Ltd.(pp 66 & 70); The poem 'Two Trees' by Don Paterson taken from 'Rain' (Faber & Faber 2010) Reproduced by permission of the author c/o Rogers, Coleridge & White Ltd.(p 67); Extracts from 'The Ferryman's Arms' by Don Paterson taken from 'Nil Nil' (Faber & Faber 1993). Reproduced by permission of the author c/o Rogers, Coleridge & White Ltd. (p 68); Extracts from 'Nil Nil' by Don Paterson taken from 'Nil Nil' (Faber & Faber 1993). Reproduced by permission of the author c/o Rogers, Coleridge & White Ltd.(p 69); Dpimborough/iStock.com (p 70); Caleb Rutherford e i d e t i c (p 71); Alexandre Duret-Lutz (p 75); The poem 'Death of a Naturalist' by Seamus Heaney, taken from the book 'Death of a Naturalist' (Faber & Faber 1966) (p 77); © RTimages/Shutterstock.com (p 84); © bzuko22 (p 87); © bzuko23 (p 87); Extract from 'Buddha Da' by Anne Donovan (Canongate Books Ltd, 2003) (p 87); Extract from 'The Crow Road' by Ian Banks (Abacus 1993) (p 96); Extact from 'Trip Trap' by Ian Rankin, from 'The Complete Short Stories: "A Good Hanging", "Beggars Banquet" (Orion 2005) (p 96); Extract from 'The Anonymous Venetian' by Donna Leon (Pan Macmillan 1995) (p 98); Art-Of-Photo/iStock.com (p 100); Petr Mika(CC BY 2.0)[3] (p 103); Nomadic Lass (CC BY-SA 2.0)[1] (p 104); Christiaan Triebert (CC BY 2.0)[3] (p 106); Pete Souza, The Obama-Biden Transition Project (CC BY 3.0)[2] (p 109); Quote from Joseph Conrad, taken from 'A Personal Record' 1919 (public domain) (p 109); Extract from Obama's acceptance speech © Whitehouse.gov (CC BY 3.0)[2] (p 109); Caleb Rutherford e i d e t i c (p 110); Extract from the BBC news article 'Staffordshire University defends its two year degrees' (http://news.bbc.co.uk/local/stoke/hi/people_and_places/newsid_9080000/9080029.stm) © BBC News (p 111); Quinn Dombrowski (CC BY-SA 2.0)[1] (p 114); Erik Charlton (CC BY 2.0)[3] (p 116); © AlexandreNunes/Shutterstock.com (p 120); © Pressmaster/Shutterstock.com (p 120); © Sergii Figurnyi/Shutterstock.com (p 120); Sean_Warren/iStock.com (p 122).

(CC BY-SA 2.0)[1] http://creativecommons.org/licenses/by-sa/2.0/
(CC BY 3.0)[2] http://creativecommons.org/licenses/by/3.0/
(CC BY 2.0)[3] http://creativecommons.org/licenses/by/2.0/

Printed and bound in the UK by Polestar Stones.

CONTENTS

INTRODUCTION

HOW THIS STUDY GUIDE WILL HELP YOU IN CfE HIGHER ENGLISH

The very fact that you're reading this suggests you are someone who takes exam success seriously. So do we!

That's why this Guide has been carefully researched and organised to bring you all the help you might need: help with simply-worded explanations of challenging concepts; help with practising how to answer exam-type questions; help with writing convincing essays of all kinds; help with listening and talking for the Units. In short, it has everything you will need to get the exam grade you are targeting.

Go through the Contents page, and you'll find there's a chapter on each of the key sections of the course. Each one will explain the guiding principles for success and then show you how to implement them in your reading, writing, listening and talking assessments.

It's a Guide with one priority: your success. Here's how it can help you achieve that.

READING FOR UNDERSTANDING, ANALYSIS AND EVALUATION

This section plays a major role in the course's final exam. So being well-versed in what to expect is vital for exam success. We'll show you how to spot examiners' expectations from the wording of the questions, what types of question to expect and, most important of all, how to approach answering them in a way that will bring you top marks. You'll find our advice explained in reader-friendly language with an answers section to guide your responses.

THE CRITICAL ESSAY

Success in critical essay writing starts long before you launch into your essay. You need to know how to read exam questions and interpret their implications. You also need to know how to plan your answer, how to structure your introduction, body paragraphs and conclusion, how to deal with quotations and how to maintain a clear flow in your essay's line of argument. All this is vital if you are to translate your reading of the text into examination success. Check out the 'Critical Essay Writing' section on the Contents page, where all the key information is broken down into easy-to-follow subsections.

THE PORTFOLIO

These are going to be two of the most important essays you have ever written. That means that in essays of up to 1300 words you have to demonstrate writing skills of the kind that will truly impress examiners. There are plenty of tips for success in this Guide to help you achieve this. These take a variety of forms. In the 'Writing Discursively' section, you'll learn how to structure, argue and persuade convincingly. In the 'Writing Creatively' section, you'll find out how to bring characters alive in a variety of ways, create atmospheric settings and construct credible plot-lines. You'll also need to think carefully about how best to present your ideas in personal and in reflective essays. We'll also talk you through what you need to consider before deciding on any one genre.

SCOTTISH TEXTS

Given that there are no fewer than 14 possible writers to study, no overall Guide can help you with all of them. We'd run out of space to cover other key areas! What we have done here, however, is to choose an author from each of the three genres – drama, prose and poetry – and show you in some detail what is happening in each text. We'll discuss areas such as character, themes and language in ways that will give you a handy model for studying other authors of your own choice. We'll also give you practice in dealing with the kind of questions you are likely to encounter in the exam itself. What's more, the three authors we have chosen – John McGrath, Janice Galloway and Don Paterson – are writers who will give you a real opportunity to demonstrate to examiners that you show some individuality and originality in your choices. Surely no bad thing when you are out to impress!

LISTENING AND TALKING

The reading and writing skills you have been acquiring elsewhere in this Guide will stand you in excellent stead to pass the Analysis and Evaluation and Creation and Production Units and thereby gain the overall course award. In this final section, we will give you practical tips and advice so that you can really stand out as a persuasive performer in the listening and talking outcomes of these Units. You'll also be able to practise on an assessment-type paper to polish your skills for the big day.

FOLLOW THE GUIDE!

So, don't feel daunted by CfE Higher English – just use this Guide. We've even made practical suggestions for some of the more extended and demanding work. And, to make the process of preparation all the easier, we've built in handy 'Don't forget' text boxes where key points are re-formed into nugget-sized reminders of essential facts and information. 'Things to do and think about' text boxes are also featured in every section. These make helpful suggestions about various preparatory exercises and study areas you might consider as you work towards achieving your best possible grade. You **can** do it!

Good luck!

READING FOR UNDERSTANDING, ANALYSIS AND EVALUATION

WHAT IS INVOLVED IN READING FOR UNDERSTANDING, ANALYSIS AND EVALUATION?

This paper represents 30 of the 70 marks in your final exam, so it is key to your overall success. To meet the challenges and gain maximum marks in this 90-minute exam, you will need to study in detail the question types you are likely to encounter and the techniques you require to answer them.

This part of the Guide is aimed at equipping you with a sound knowledge of the question types you should expect and the expertise you require to come up with top-grade answers. First, we'll explain what will be required of you. Then we'll set about familiarising you with how to respond successfully to questions. Finally, we'll give you some practice in putting this knowledge to work effectively.

Let's get started.

WHAT ARE THE LIKELY TEXTS?

The texts will be examples of detailed and complex non-fiction writing selected from areas such as serious journalism, travel writing and biography. You will be required to read two texts on a similar topic, answer questions on the first text and then, in a final question, compare the two texts in a way specified by the examiner.

It makes sense to familiarise yourself with such texts as early as possible, because although they will introduce you to many interesting topics, the richness of their expression can be challenging and their ideas thought-provoking, and getting to grips with these for the first time in the examination room probably isn't the best idea! Make sure you put aside time to read quality newspapers and magazines regularly, so that when you sit the exam, you will be familiar with the vocabulary and structures of good-quality, non-fiction writing.

And doing this will also help your own writing.

MAKING THE BEST START

Time is always short in the exam room, but time spent reading – intelligently – will pay real dividends in the quality of your answers. The intelligent reader adopts a two-stage approach.

THE FIRST READ

Check out any information in the rubric at the top of the passage: there may be a clue there as to the writer's attitude to the topic; this may help with later questions on tone. Then, read the first sentence of each paragraph to get a feel for the flow of the passage. A sense of where the text is going is often vital to picking up the writer's overall intentions. Is a question set out at the start and then systematically answered in the various paragraphs?

For example:

Firstly ... In the second place ...

or

In earliest times ... The Romans later ... Latterly ...

Is there a balanced argument, with the writer changing direction mid-way? Or is there some tie-up between an opening statement and a concluding one? Whatever approach the

contd

author has selected, the first sentence in each paragraph will help to give you a strategic overview of the approach adopted and its direction of travel. Always be alert to seemingly inconsequential words and phrases like **however**, **but**, **nevertheless**, **whereas**, **in spite of** and **similarly**: they are invaluable for signalling upcoming shifts in the writer's stance.

THE SECOND READ

Now that you have an **informed** sense of the writer's overall intentions, you can settle down to absorb the passage's detail. Some people like to read through the entire passage again, marking up key points as they go before tackling the questions; others like to work on analysing the sense of individual paragraphs and then answering their related questions. A thorough second reading of the text, however managed, will be really helpful in appreciating the passage's complexity of ideas and richness of language features. (But do keep an eye on the time.) Only with this alertness will you pick up top marks.

WHAT KIND OF QUESTIONS SHOULD I EXPECT?

You will need to be able to answer questions that test your skills in understanding, analysing and evaluating the texts in front of you.

The number of marks allocated to each question will be clearly marked, which will help you to manage your time appropriately.

But first, let's take a brief overview of the range of questions you will need to be able to answer.

QUESTIONS TESTING UNDERSTANDING SKILLS

In Higher English, testing understanding can take various forms. Some understanding questions will probe your factual understanding of key points or expressions; some will ask you to summarise certain key points; some will ask you to suggest what the writer is implying but not stating outright at certain points. In all cases, however, the emphasis is always on you being able to articulate a response using **your own words** wherever possible. You must avoid 'lifting' vocabulary or expressions from the passages.

QUESTIONS TESTING ANALYSIS SKILLS

Here the challenge is rather different. Now you are being asked to analyse **how** a writer is making language work to achieve a certain effect. Good writers can use a variety of techniques to achieve their effect. What specific techniques have been used in this instance? Word choice? Sentence structure? Figurative language? Here you will need to point to specific examples from the passage, identify how they work in the writer's hands and suggest what the effect on the reader is.

QUESTIONS TESTING EVALUATION SKILLS

These ask you for your opinion of **how well** you think something has been said. To do this, you will need to find examples from the passage to back up your evaluation. You might point to a particularly successful simile, for instance, or a balanced sentence that gets an idea across memorably, or a striking contrast in the choice of words: such examples will form the basis of your comment. You might well have commented on these already in an analysis question, but now you need to go further and give your personal 'take' on them. How well did these items help get the writer's overall intentions across, **in your opinion**? Be prepared to interrogate your own feelings and say what they are.

 DON'T FORGET

Before beginning your answer, check out how many marks are being awarded for it. Allocate your time appropriately.

 ONLINE

Try clicking the link to the *Scotsman* at www.brightredbooks.net, and then tap on the *Scotsman* strapline at the top of the page. Scroll down to 'Opinion' and 'Comment' pieces, which deal with issues of the day. These are the basis of many close reading articles.

 THINGS TO DO AND THINK ABOUT

Regular reading of quality newspapers such as the *Scotsman*, the *Herald*, the *Guardian*, the *Independent* and so on will do much to boost your performance not only in Reading for Understanding, Analysis and Evaluation but also in discursive portfolio work. Remember that you can also read many of the quality journals online.

 ONLINE TEST

How well have you learned this topic? Take the test at www.brightredbooks.net

UNDERSTANDING: AN OVERVIEW

SHOWING YOU UNDERSTAND

The aim here is to assess what you have derived from your reading. In other words, have you understood what the writer is getting at? You are expected to be able to understand the key points the writer is making and, at times, to summarise them. You are also expected to demonstrate your understanding by suggesting what the writer is also saying 'between the lines'.

Often, an understanding question will ask you to **identify** something the writer has commented on: for example, a reason, feeling, purpose, claim or fear. Or it might ask you to use your own words to **explain** or say **in what ways** two people or things are different or similar, making the relationship between them clear.

It's essential to remember that whether you are summarising, inferring meaning or simply showing understanding, you must do all this **in your own words**. 'Lifting' words or expressions from the texts is a sure-fire way to lose marks. Examiners argue that you do not understand any concept until you can express it in your own words.

USING YOUR OWN WORDS

Don't be tempted to try to do a word-for-word 'translation' of the idea. This doesn't usually work because you are not a thesaurus and don't always have a word that means exactly the same as the original at your disposal. It's much better to explain the idea in your own way than to grope about for words that mean approximately the same.

For instance, suppose a key idea to be expressed in your own words was: In the last few years, we've moved from an information-scarce economy to one driven by

DO I CHANGE EVERYTHING?

No. There will be certain words which common sense dictates need to be left as they are. Proper nouns and common nouns with no obvious alternatives (for example, *tripod*, *breathalyser* and *leopard*) should remain as they are.

an information glut. (From 'Why our future depends on libraries, reading and daydreaming', Neil Gaiman, in the *Guardian*, 15 October 2013.) While *'In the last few years'* is fairly straightforward, looking for time-consuming alternative adjectives and nouns to *information-scarce economy* or *information glut* might be tricky. Try expressing the idea in quite another way: 'Once, our commercial world didn't have enough data to work with. Nowadays, it seems we have too much.'

Verbs, adverbs, adjectives and all figurative language (for example, *prices have rocketed*) will need to be rephrased in your own words.

TRACKING DOWN THE ANSWER

In questions seeking to test your understanding, a two-stage approach might be helpful.

- Stage 1: Highlight or underline the words or phrases in which you feel the answer is to be found. This will focus your attention on the required information and will help you to steer clear of unintentional 'lifts' when you

come to expressing your answer in your own words.
- Stage 2: Work out how best to re-fashion the key idea in your own way, perhaps not by 'shadowing' the sequence of words but by looking for another starting point entirely.

SUMMARISING INFORMATION

We'll cover summarising information in more detail when we come to discuss the high-value questions in your Reading for Understanding, Analysis and Evaluation paper, which is where this skill will probably prove most useful. For the moment, we're going to look at what this skill entails and discuss some strategies for reducing text to key points.

contd

Your understanding of a passage is not complete unless you can confidently summarise its key points. And once again, you must be able to do this in your own words. Avoid 'lifting' words and expressions at all costs, although, as with 'understanding' questions, you can retain technical terms, proper nouns and common nouns with no alternatives.

The skill required here is to reduce the identified passage to its essential message, cutting out interesting but non-essential detail. You need to know what to remove.

So, what should you leave out?
- figurative language such as metaphors and similes
- examples
- lists
- detailed statistical information
- comparisons.

Then in your own words you have to summarise, as briefly as possible, what remains. Check the question itself for guidance on what is required to be summarised. E.g. *Summarise key points the writer makes about living in Venice.*

LET'S TRY THAT OUT

Here is a brief text and summarising exercise on the Scottish writer, Eric Linklater.

> Write a short summary which makes key points about Linklater and his place in Scottish literature. *(Tip: read text for key points, note them down in your own words, organise them into a text of your own.)*

> Eric Linklater (1899–1974) was one of the most prolific writers of his generation. With twenty-three novels, three collections of short stories, half a dozen plays, a volume of poems, two children's novels and an impressive list of biographies, essays and histories to his credit, his place in the canon of Scottish literature might be assumed to be an assured one. But although highly popular with the public in the 1930s and the 1940s, Linklater's style of novel began to fall out of fashion as early as the 1950s, at a time when the post-war generation of novelists began to monopolise the attention of literary critics.

(from Christopher Nicol, *Eric Linklater's 'Private Angelo' and 'The Dark of Summer'*, ASLS, Glasgow 2012)

 ## THINGS TO DO AND THINK ABOUT

Now, looking at the text and instructions on how to go about summarising, to which of these Linklater summaries would you award 5 marks? Justify your answer by referring closely to each answer. Award a mark for each key point. Point out where guidelines have been ignored.

> Born in 1899 and dying in 1974, Eric Linklater wrote 23 novels as well as many other kinds of books. All these books were highly popular while he was alive, but, as he got older, people didn't like his work so much, and the literary critics began to like the post-war generation of novelists more.

> Working in a variety of genres, twentieth-century writer Eric Linklater produced such a wealth of works that we might think he would be well remembered after his death. But public enthusiasm for his work in the first half of the century later declined, and commentators began to favour younger writers.

> Although he was popular when he was a young man, Eric Linklater later fell out of favour with the public and critics, despite his many novels, plays, biographies and histories. The critics now began to turn their attention to younger writers from the post-war generation of novelists.

INFERENCE-MAKING

1983

2013

AN INTRODUCTION TO INFERENCE-MAKING

Going about our daily business, we make inferences all the time. Often these inferences are instinctive: we see an ambulance outside a shop, so we infer that someone has fallen ill. Often we make inferences from visual clues. What, for instance, can we infer is being said about electronic technology from this cartoon?

In written texts, the process is much the same. In texts, we make inferences when we 'read between the lines', looking this time for verbal information which the author is suggesting but not saying outright. Inference-making questions belong among understanding questions, since they test what we have understood from the text. But they have something in common with analysis-type questions, too, since we need to find textual evidence to back up what we have inferred. Look at this short text:

> 'Oh,' cried Rachel, 'the tree is so beautiful. I love the new coloured lights. And just look at the star Carol bought for the top. Leave the curtains open so everyone can see it!'

Without actually mentioning the word *Christmas,* it is clear from the textual evidence we pick up that the period is Christmas and the tree in question is a Christmas tree: *coloured lights, star [...] for the top*; and the tree occupies a position in the window, fairly typical of such trees. So, we have inferred the period in question without being told directly by the writer that it is Christmas. And we can also infer that Rachel is proud of her tree since she wants the curtains left open.

There are various inferences that we can be expected to pick up on:

- **Inferences about factual information** (as above)
- **Inferences about a person's feelings or emotions** (as above)
- **Inferences about the author's attitude towards a topic or person**
- **Inferences about the meanings of specific words.**

Inferences can often be detected from:

- **Factual clues** (here: coloured lights, stars, window position, open curtains)
- **Word-choice connotations**
- **Imagery connotations.**

 **ACTIVITY** UNDERSTANDING QUESTIONS

Let's now see how we can put that information to work by looking at some basic understanding questions.

1 Charles Montgomery examines a slightly surprising link between happiness and one man's location.

> When we talk about cities, we usually end up talking about how various places look, and perhaps how it feels to be there. But to stop there misses half the story, because the way we experience most parts of cities is at velocity: we glide past on the way to somewhere else. City life is as much about moving through landscapes as it is about being in them. Robert Judge, a 48-year-old husband and father, once wrote to a Canadian radio show explaining how much he enjoyed going grocery shopping on his bicycle. Judge's confession would have

DON'T FORGET

You can often infer the meaning of a difficult word in a close reading passage by examining its context, e.g. *We argued all day with her but she was deaf to our arguments, remaining totally* <u>*intransigent*</u>. The context suggests she could not be moved by our arguments, hence *intransigent* means unshakeable/unyielding/ stubborn.

contd

been unremarkable if he did not happen to live in Saskatoon, Saskatchewan, where the average temperature in January hovers around -17°C. The city stays frozen and snowy for almost half the year. Judge's pleasure in an experience that seems slower, more difficult and considerably more uncomfortable than the alternative might seem bizarre. He explained it by way of a story: sometimes, he said, he would pick up his three-year-old son from nursery and put him on the back seat of his tandem bike and they would pedal home along the South Saskatchewan river. The snow would muffle the noise of the city. Dusk would paint the sky in colours so exquisite that Judge could not begin to find names for them. The snow would reflect those hues. It would glow like the sky, and Judge would breathe in the cold air and hear his son breathing behind him, and he would feel as though together they had become part of winter itself.

(From Charles Montgomery, *Happy City: Transforming Our Lives Through Urban Design*, Penguin Press, London 2013)

a   Explain in your own words what the writer means by 'City life is as much about moving through landscapes as it is about being in them.'   **3**
b   What inference can you make here about the writer's views on cycle rides? Point to evidence to support your answer.   **3**
c   Summarise in your own words five benefits Judge derived from his cycle ride. You may answer this question in continuous prose or in a series of bullet points.   **5**

2

There was a moment early last week when both the BBC and Sky were dedicating the full resources of their 24-hour news output to a reportedly biblical deluge that had apparently wiped out much of the west of England. "At that moment," says one police officer, "precisely 10 dwellings were affected by the floods. Of those, just seven were flooded, and five of those seven were occupied."

(From Peter Oborne, 'Yes, the floods are awful, but we must keep a sense of proportion', in the *Daily Telegraph*, 12 February 2014)

a   What inference can be drawn here as to the writer's opinion of British news coverage? Suggest textual evidence to support your answer.   **3**

3

Eric Linklater (1899–1974) was one of the most prolific writers of his generation. With twenty-three novels, three collections of short stories, half a dozen plays, a volume of poems, two children's novels and an impressive list of biographies, essays and histories to his credit, his place in the canon of Scottish literature might be assumed to be an assured one. But although highly popular with the public in the 1930s and the 1940s, Linklater's style of novel began to fall out of fashion as early as the 1950s, at a time when the post-war generation of novelists began to monopolise the attention of literary critics.

(from Christopher Nicol, *Eric Linklater's 'Private Angelo' and 'The Dark of Summer'*, ASLS, Glasgow 2012)

a   Explain in your own words the phrase 'the post-war generation of novelists began to monopolise the attention of literary critics'.   **3**
b   What does the writer seem to be implying about writers with large outputs of work? Support your answer with textual evidence.   **3**

 THINGS TO DO AND THINK ABOUT

Take time to do a first and second reading of all three questions above before answering. You can check your answers on page 124.

ANALYSING WORD CHOICE

DON'T FORGET

If you are asked to 'analyse how' the writer conveys information or 'refer to X features of the writer's use of language', you need to find and comment on how specific examples of language are used in the passage. This is a question about how effects are created, not explaining meaning.

ANALYSING LANGUAGE

By analysing language, you are saying how writers manipulate language to create certain effects on their readers. Your answer needs to pinpoint the techniques employed to this end and then discuss how they influence readers. Usually these techniques can be found under four broad headings:

- word choice
- imagery
- structure/punctuation
- tone

Before exploring these headings, let's see how to tackle a question that requires you to analyse the writer's language.

HOW DO I ANALYSE?

There are three basic steps to follow:

1 Locate specific words or phrases from the text for your answer, for example:
   bible black ... pale as death ...
   alive, she was worshipped; dead, she was demonised ...
2 Identify which technique the author is using – for example: metaphor, simile or balanced sentence/parallel structure – unless, of course, the question already specifies which technique you are asked to discuss.
3 Explain in your own words **how** this specific use of language works on the reader. What effect is it having? What you say here will depend on the category of language you are discussing.

Each of the four categories mentioned above generally follows this three-part process, but each has its differences. We'll look at them all in turn.

WORD CHOICE

Probably without being aware of it, we have certain ideas about specific words hardwired into our brains. Words tend to have associations or **connotations** for us, which word-choice questions exploit to the full. Nouns, adjectives, verbs and adverbs usually carry with them more than a dictionary definition or **denotation**.

For example, look at the following two words. They are both concerned with asking someone to do something, but they each have very different connotations:

To demand: here pressure is being put on the listener to do something. The speaker appears to believe he/she is in a position of strength.

To plead: here the speaker appears to be in a weak position. Far from being in a situation of strength, he/she is begging the listener to do something.

If the question asks about the language of a particular section, and you feel it is rich in words with interesting connotations, word-choice comments could be part of your overall answer. Remember that 'language' could also include imagery or sentence structure.

Use your highlighter to emphasise non-neutral words or expressions that leap out at you from the text. The process is straightforward:

- Locate the word(s).
- Explore the connotations the word(s) has for you and perhaps contrast this word(s) with a more neutral term to sharpen the difference.
- Say why this word is effective in this context.

contd

Jamie Oliver definitely widened the appeal of cooking when he arrived on telly branded as the Naked Chef: a young bloke chucking pasta around in his trendy warehouse flat, playing in a band, and speeding off on his Vespa.

(From Sophie Heawood, 'It's not enough to be a celebrity brand. Today you must be a guru', in the *Guardian*, 1 January 2014)

1 Show how the writer's word choice emphasises how Oliver wants to be seen as being very ordinary. **3**

Let's pick out individual words or expressions that suggest the everyday nature of Oliver and his lifestyle. This question is worth three marks, so remember that you can obtain two marks for a detailed/insightful comment plus a quote or reference, and one mark for a more basic comment plus a quote/reference. (If you can't find three examples, give as full an explanation of your chosen word(s) as you can.)

Here's an example of a three-mark answer.

'bloke': the colloquial term for a young man suggests Jamie is no-one special. 'bloke' rather than 'young man' suggests he is just 'one of the lads'.
'chucking [pasta]': the colloquial 'chucking' rather than the more neutral 'throwing' suggests typically 'laddish' behaviour rather than perhaps the more conventional treatment of pasta associated with TV chefs.
'[on his] Vespa': travelling around London on a humble scooter rather than in a more upmarket vehicle suggests a picture of non-celebrity, man-in-the-street behaviour.

 ACTIVITY WORD CHOICE

Now you try an example on your own. The questions that follow this extract ask you to analyse use of language generally, but for this activity concentrate on analysing word choice.

Here, James Harkin considers how electronic communications appear to be dehumanising our relationships.

Like Joseph Weizenbaum, Professor Sherry Turkle has undergone a conversion from early digital utopian to wary digital realist. In her controversial new book *Alone Together: Why we expect more from technology and less from each other*, she argues that we've 'invented ways of being with people that turn them into something close to objects'.

  Instead of conversing on the phone we send a text; rather than nurturing friendships we fire off Facebook messages, or computer-generated aides memoire of acquaintances' birthdays. Tempted by the prospect of keeping in touch with many different people at once, she writes, we're turning away from real human relationships and towards a relentless cycle of sending out cursory messages and responding to inane feedback. Far from freeing up more time to see our real friends, it's made our communication more rote, our relationships a little robotic.

(From James Harkin, 'Living in Cyburbia', in the *Telegraph*, 29 January 2011)

1 Analyse James Harkin's language in the first paragraph. How does it show that Sherry Turkle's views on electronic communications have changed? **4**

2 In the second paragraph, show how Turkle's use of language makes clear the contrast she sees between real friendship and what is replacing it. **4**

 DON'T FORGET

Remember that in this paper you don't need to write your answers in sentences. As in the example above, you can select your word(s), put it (them) in inverted commas, add a colon and then begin your unpacking of connotations. Depending on the context, you could also compare the writer's word with a more neutral word.

 THINGS TO DO AND THINK ABOUT

In class or with a partner, discuss the connotations of the following strings of words:

elephantine	obese	chubby	sturdy	overweight
grudgingly	slyly	furtively	cautiously	unwillingly
lurk	wait	linger	loiter	lounge

 ONLINE

For more on analysing word choice, follow the link at www.brightredbooks.net

IMAGERY

IMAGERY: AN OVERVIEW

Like word choice, imagery is another device used by writers to create vivid pictures and associations in our minds. It is also something you need to consider seriously when the question asks you to consider the writer's 'language'.

As with other analysis-type questions, any analysis of imagery needs to adopt the three-part response:

1 Locate relevant words or phrases from the text, for example:
   eyes like marbles ...
2 Identify the particular device you see at work – for example: simile, metaphor, personification or alliteration – unless the question has already identified this device for comment.
3 Explain how the imagery helps to convey the writer's intention to the reader, for example:
   'In the same way that marbles are attractive but hard, her eyes are beautiful, but unyielding and lacking in warmth.'

Imagery comes under the umbrella of 'figurative language' devices. A sound knowledge of the various figurative language devices and how writers apply them is vital for tackling questions in every section of the course, as well as in your critical essay.

There are two broad categories: those which conjure up visual images, and those which create sound – or aural – images.

VISUAL IMAGERY/DEVICES	AURAL IMAGERY/DEVICES
Simile: a comparison between two items using 'like' or 'as': *He's like a dog with a bone.* The effect of similes and metaphors is to add visual emphasis/impact to the written description.	**Alliteration:** the repetition of a particular consonant – or consonant sound – at the beginning of a group of words to create a certain sound effect: *Cold clay clads his coffin.* Here the harsh sound of the letter 'c' matches the grimness of the description. *Soft sighing of the southern seas.* Here the soft 's' sounds mimics the gentleness of the water's sound.
Metaphor: also a comparison, but this time the two items being compared are not 'like' each other, since one item becomes the other: *You're an angel.*	**Assonance:** the repetition of a certain group of similar-sounding vowels in words close to each other, again used to create a certain aural effect: *And murmuring of innumerable bees.*
Personification: yet another way of making a comparison. Similes and metaphors can become examples of personification when an inanimate object (without life) is spoken of as if it were human and alive: *And moonbeams kiss the sea.*	**Onomatopoeia:** here the sound of the word mimics its meaning: *Clink, fizz, rip, honk, boom, purr* suggest their meaning in their sound.
Hyperbole: an exaggerated image to create a certain effect (often humorous) or to emphasise something: *The list goes on for miles.* *He never fails to get lost.*	**Enjambment:** in poetry, this is the running-on of one line into another or into several others, often to give either a conversational feel to the content or sometimes to suggest a speeding-up for an effect of urgency. It also creates a feeling of suspense because the reader has to wait until the end of the line, couplet or stanza for the key point to be made: *... for my purpose holds* *To sail beyond the sunset, and the baths* *Of all the western stars, until I die.*

When dealing with similes, metaphors and personification, which make comparisons between two items, you need to think about what the items have in common before commenting on the effectiveness of the chosen example. For instance, an icicle is cold and hard, a lion is bold, a warm bath is comforting. Here's an example:

Just as an icicle is hard and cold, so, too, was their aunt's smile in that it was similarly brittle and lacking warmth.

contd

ACTIVITY ANALYSIS QUESTIONS

Using only your knowledge of **imagery** and **word choice**, try these activities.

In Venice, Jan Morris reflects on the contrasts evident in the shipping Basin of St Mark during the day and later at night.

> Nothing is more stimulating, on a gleaming spring day, than the kaleidoscopic Basin of St Mark, the pool that lies directly before the Piazzetta. In the day-time the basin is never calm, however still the weather, because of the constant churning of ships and propellers: but at night, if you take your boat out there through the lamplight, it is as still and dark and luscious as a great lake of plum-juice, through which your bows seep thickly, and into whose sickly viscous liquid the dim shape of the Doge's Palace seems to be slowly sinking, like a pastry pavilion.

(From Jan Morris, *Venice*, Faber and Faber, London, 1993)

1 Choose any two examples of the language used to convey the night-time character of the basin's water, and analyse how each example is effective in conveying this character. **4**

2 By referring to two features of language, analyse how the writer makes the precarious position of the Doge's Palace apparent. **4**

James Harkin considers how audiences for books and television are changing in their taste and demands.

> The most fetching book I've come across for ages wasn't in a traditional bookshop but on a recent visit to the South London Gallery in Peckham. It was Thackeray's *Vanity Fair,* but not the Penguin Popular Classic. This one was pale pink and as big as a box, newly typeset, accompanied by 30 gorgeous illustrations. So, even as the big beasts of publishing struggle, and their traditional retailers lurch from crisis to crisis, there are reasons to be hopeful. Some publishers are doing well by producing objects beautiful enough to be collectible. That *Vanity Fair* I saw is from Four Corners Books, a tiny east London publisher with two employees; as well as new books, Four Corners knocks out "Familiars" by inviting contemporary artists to create fresh editions of classic novels and short stories.
>
> But it isn't only the book that is changing its form. Many of us, it turns out, don't now want to spend all our time consuming random gobbets of electronic information. We're hungry for longer things to get our teeth into – as new things sprout up in different shapes and sizes, our diet is growing more diverse. The same people who snack on bite-sized nuggets of online video at work might revel in a long HBO serial like The Wire an episode at a time in the evening, a richer diet than anything they're likely to encounter on mainstream TV. Just as novels evolved in the 19th century to cope with the demands of newspaper serialisation, television is liberating itself from stale old formats and stretching out into sprawling, more intricate kinds of story.

(From James Harkin, 'A whole new e-chapter', in the *Guardian*, 26 April 2011)

1 From the first paragraph, analyse how the writer makes it clear that questions of size are leading to contrasting fortunes in the book trade. **4**

2 In the second paragraph, analyse:
   a how the writer uses language to reinforce the contrast between present and past viewing preferences **4**
   b how the writer contrasts casual viewing habits with more serious viewing. **4**

3 Read the final sentence. Analyse the image the writer uses here to convey his attitude to the development he notes. **2**

 THINGS TO DO AND THINK ABOUT

Before you check your answers on page 125, check you have respected the time-saving, mark-winning three-part formula: locate items, identify them and explain their effect on the reader. Remember, too, that you don't need to write your answers in sentences.

 ONLINE TEST

Want to revise your knowledge of this? Head to www.brightredbooks.net and take the test.

 ONLINE

For more information about how to analyse imagery, head to www.brightredbooks.net

DON'T FORGET

You will need a knowledge of figurative language for at least three areas of your final exam. Can you say in which areas this knowledge will prove useful?

DON'T FORGET

When dealing with similes, metaphors and personification (which are essentially about comparisons), remember to say what **links** the two things being compared. A useful formula to consider is: *Just as a … is …, so, too, is a … in that it is also…*

SENTENCE STRUCTURE/PUNCTUATION 1

So far, we have looked at how writers create effects with word choice and imagery **within** the sentence. Now we need to look at how writers create their effect with the **sentence itself** and with the punctuation that helps structure the sentence.

We're looking at sentence structure and punctuation together because they are so interlinked. In fact, one of the building blocks of sentence structure is punctuation, so we'll look at this first.

DON'T FORGET

Understanding punctuation marks can help you in a variety of question types in your Reading for Understanding, Analysis and Evaluation paper. For example, a colon can signal a qualification or an explanation that will help you understand more fully what the writer is saying; depending on where it comes in the sentence. Ellipsis can suggest an interruption, indecision, anticipation or suspense, and will therefore hint about the writer's state of mind. Exclamation marks can indicate a particular tone which will help you to evaluate a writer's stance on a topic.

EXAMINING PUNCTUATION

Don't underestimate how useful it is to know and understand the main features of punctuation when you are asked to discuss the 'language' of the author. For example, one extract might feature a series of sentences all ending with a question mark, suggesting a character's bewilderment. Another extract might feature a series of words around which the writer has inserted inverted commas, signalling that the writer is casting doubt on their surface meaning. Punctuation marks perform a whole range of useful purposes in a writer's text; knowing the ones you are likely to encounter is a basic part of your examination preparation.

Here are some of the more common punctuation marks. You really need to know what they are and how they contribute to sentence structure if you want to be able to explore how authors use them to create effects with their writing.

TYPE OF PUNCTUATION	PUNCTUATION MARK	USE
Full stop	•	Its position indicates the completion of a sentence. The position of the full stop determines whether we are dealing with long or short sentences and, as you'll find out in the next section, how each is used to different effect.
Comma	,	Usually used to separate brief items in a list: *Apples, pears, bananas and a grapefruit.* Used before and after a phrase, commas are said to be used as parenthesis markers. *Enter Arthur, a distant cousin, in love with Anne.* The phrase *a distant cousin* is said to be in parenthesis. When you are answering a question, you could say: 'The phrase in parenthesis adds additional information about ...' See also pairs of dashes and brackets below.
Semi-colon	;	Often used to separate larger items in a list: *A beach house in Bermuda; a flat in Paris, on the Champs Elysées no less; a chalet in the Alps; a castle in Scotland with over 40 rooms: all these were owned by their aunt.* They also indicate a turning point in a balanced sentence: *Sober, he was unpredictable; drunk, he was dangerous.* *To err is human; to forgive divine.*
Colon	:	A colon can signal an explanation or elaboration that is to follow: *It was now night: stars twinkled overhead and the moon was rising.* Or it can signal an upcoming quotation: *Criticised for being harsh, Les replies: 'Heart like a flint, that's me.'* It can also introduce a list: *Her garden was a picture: marigolds, lupins, roses, daisies and, in spring, masses of tulips.*

contd

Dashes and brackets	— — ( )	Pairs of dashes, brackets or commas on either side of a phrase – *her mother's cousin* – are used to create what we call a phrase *in parenthesis*. When you are answering a question, you could say 'The phrase in parenthesis adds additional information about ...'
		An individual dash can be used to add emphasis or importance to a word or phrase following it:
		And there it lay before them, glittering in the blue Aegean – Hydra.
		An individual dash can sometimes also be used as a kind of informal colon, indicating a concluding list or explanation:
		He had taken great trouble over their evening meal – prawns, roast venison and a fine raspberry tart.
Ellipsis	• • •	In mid-sentence, these three dots can be used to suggest an interruption, hesitation or indecision. Used at the end of the sentence, they can suggest anticipation or suspense:
		The door opened and a hand appeared ...
Exclamation mark	!	Usually used to indicate strong emotion on the part of the writer: often surprise, excitement or anger:
		It was Bill!
Question mark	?	This is used to indicate a question, which in turn can be used as a structuring device for that section of the article – for example, the writer asks a question and then proceeds to answer it in the following paragraph.
		Alternatively, the writer can ask a series of questions to signal confusion or bewilderment:
		Who could she turn to? Was there anyone she could trust? What if they were all against her?
		Or sometimes a question mark can be used to create a rhetorical question, which invites readers to share the writer's views:
		What kind of society turns its back on those in need? You need to say precisely what the apparent aim of the writer is – for example: *... to win the reader's support for his views on what constitutes a just society ...*
Inverted commas (quotation marks)	' '	When they are used around an individual word or phrase, inverted commas suggest that the writer is casting doubt on the surface meaning of the word:
		I had little faith in the 'help' being offered by the bank. Here the writer is indicating that the 'help' is so-called help, rather than real assistance. Quotation marks are also used to indicate the title of a poem, a song, an article or a chapter in a book. (The title of a book, a film or a play is usually typeset in italics in print form, but when you are writing them by hand, you could use underlining or perhaps quotation marks.)

ONLINE TEST

Head to www.brightredbooks.net and take the test on this section.

 THINGS TO DO AND THINK ABOUT

To get you thinking about punctuation before you start analysing texts themselves, try some practical exercises on the subject. Key 'Punctuation Marks Exercise – University of Bristol' into a search engine online and work through the questions. This is a useful way to familiarise yourself with the more common punctuation marks.

 ## ONLINE

Check out the link at www.brightredbooks.net to practise your punctuation skills.

SENTENCE STRUCTURE/PUNCTUATION 2

We have looked at the role punctuation plays in shaping individual sentences. Good writers will use these to the full, but they will also use other shaping techniques that you will need to be familiar with.

IDENTIFYING FEATURES OF SENTENCE STRUCTURE

So, what shaping techniques are available to a good writer? Here are some examples:

SENTENCE TYPE	USE
Long sentences	Used to suggest the sheer length of something, a route of a river or road, for example, or the complexity of a process, or the boredom of something dragging on and on.
Short sentences	Used to intensify the impact/drama of what is being said. A brief remark in a sentence can create a very dramatic effect: *And with that, she left.* Many forms of persuasive writing (such as advertising) make use of the short sentence: *Try it. You'll love it. Every woman does.* A short sentence that follows a particularly long one can be very powerful: the dramatic impact is heightened even more.
A list (neutral, with climax or anti-climax)	Used to underline/emphasise/highlight the sheer number of items, actions or people being described. Always check lists out for additional possibilities. It might build to a **climax**: *She had played hostess to generals, princes, kings and even the mighty Napoleon himself.* This is a technique which adds to the impact of the final item. It might, however, end in an **anti-climax**: *His case contained a pair of Gucci loafers, a Rolex watch, cologne by Chanel and a pair of dirty underpants.* This technique is often used for humorous effect. Of course, it might just simply be a neutral list! But it's a sound idea to check out any list for climax or anti-climax.
Sentences without verbs	These are known as minor sentences. Sometimes they create a chatty, informal effect: *Great! Another fine mess. What next?* Or, as with the short sentences described above, they can be used to add dramatic impact: *A woman's glove. Slightly blood-stained.*

contd

Word order	Normal word order in English tends to follow this pattern:
	He was fierce in his claim to innocence.
	But, to emphasise/underline/highlight a certain element in the sentence, the writer can invert the normal order, and place the important word(s) first:
	Fierce he was in his claim to innocence.
	But the inversion can also be manipulated so that the important word that the writer wants to emphasise is placed at the end:
	In his claim to innocence he was fierce.
	Exam tip: if you cannot see anything at all in a sentence to comment on, check out inversion. It is often one of the last things we think of. And it *might* just be the right answer!
Repetition	This may take the form of repeated words or phrases to underline/intensify the idea the writer is seeking to emphasise at a particular point:
	A good cyclist needs ... A good cyclist hopes that ... But a good cyclist knows above all that ...
	Note that these repetitions in the closing stages of a text might be building to a climax. It is worth mentioning in your answer if you detect this.
Balanced sentences	When writers wish to make us strongly aware of some contrast that they want to indicate, they sometimes resort to these. They are recognisable by the semi-colon (;) that acts as a pivot, or balancing point, in the middle of the sentence:
	Alive, she had been seen as a saint; dead, she was quickly demonised.
Rhetorical question	These are questions that expect no direct answer. Rather, it is the writer's way of trying to get the reader to support their views.
	Who wants to see a child suffer in this way?
	Here the reader is expected to share the writer's horror at the ill-treatment of children.
Parallel structures	These are patterns of either phrases or words which give a pleasing predictability and rhythm to the sentence. The effect is to add emphasis to what is being said:
	It is by logic we prove, but by intuition we discover (da Vinci).
	The ants were everywhere: climbing *over jampots,* swarming *under the sink,* scrambling *into cupboards,* diving *into the bin.*
	The likeness of pattern here (verb + preposition+ noun) makes for a more memorable phrase and creates a greater impact than a less patterned structure would.

DON'T FORGET

You need to know all these sentence-structuring techniques by heart before you go into the exam room; you won't have time to search your memory for them. Highlight them and memorise them – now!

ONLINE

Learn more about sentence structure by following the link at www.brightredbooks.net

ONLINE TEST

How well have you learned this topic? Take the test at www.brightredbooks.net

THINGS TO DO AND THINK ABOUT

As part of your regular reading of the quality press, study the papers' use of sentence structuring for special effects, particularly in their 'Leader', 'Comment' or 'Opinion' pieces. Remember this information when you come to your own writing. In argumentative and persuasive essays, masterful use of varied sentence-structuring devices can add a powerful dimension to your line of argument. Use them to the full.

SENTENCE STRUCTURE/PUNCTUATION 3

In your exam, the questions in the Reading for Understanding, Analysis and Evaluation section will usually be quite broad in their wording, inviting you, for instance, to discuss the writer's language or to analyse how he/she creates certain effects. In your answer sentence structure/punctuation may well be the only one of these items you will discuss as part of your overall answer. But don't forget to check out the possible contribution of imagery, word choice or tone as well.

⚙ ACTIVITY SENTENCE STRUCTURE/PUNCTUATION

We want to give you some practice in answering questions about sentence structure. So, when you read and respond to the following three extracts, concentrate on analysing how the three writers use this technique to create certain effects. But remember that this is a practice test, and that you'll have to analyse **all** the writer's language techniques in the exam – not just sentence structure.

Here, a man of the Night Watch in George R. R. Martin's A Clash of Kings *swears his loyalty oath.*

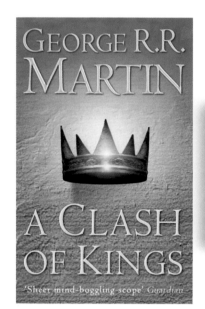

> Night gathers, and now my watch begins. It shall not end until my death. I shall take no wife, hold no lands, father no children. I shall wear no crowns and win no glory. I shall live and die at my post. I am the sword in the darkness. I am the watcher on the walls. I am the fire that burns against the cold, the light that brings the dawn, the horn that wakes the sleepers, the shield that guards the realms of men. I pledge my life and honour to the Night's Watch, for this night and all the nights to come.

(From George R. R. Martin, *A Clash of Kings*, Voyager, 1999)

1   How does the writer's language in this paragraph add impact to the sworn dedication of the men of the Night Watch?   **4**

In this passage, the writer describes the neighbourhood in which she was born and grew up.

> Glendale Street seemed to me, a ten-year-old then, to go on for ever: first you came on the row of dowdy shops selling dreary goods that never seemed to be bought, followed by the even grimmer series of tall tenements whose permanent grey shadow never seemed to lift, then came the windowless walls of Lewis & Keith's foundry, belching vile fumes that never seemed to disperse. But then there was the park.
>
> In the spring a carpet of crocuses sprang up as if by magic – yellow, white, purple. At Easter, we and our eggs rolled down the grassy slopes, shrieking with delight – well, we did, not our eggs – before banging into the green-painted benches by the pond. Why is it that our imaginations block out the grimness of childhood? How is it that our memory retains the pleasure of youth?

contd

1   In what ways does the writer's language suggest (a) the seemingly endless nature of the street? (b) its unchanging nature?   **6**

2   How does the writer's use of language in the first paragraph add significance to the park in her memory?   **2**

3   How does the writer's language in paragraph two seek to win our acceptance of her views on our early years?   **4**

This passage describes Harry's journey from the sports centre.

There it was again. Harry stopped and listened. That was three times now. Frost glistened like thousands of diamonds on the pavement as he stood there, motionless. His breath drifted up like cigarette smoke in the cold night sky. Tap, tap. Was it footsteps he was hearing? No. It was more like a stick. Yes, a walking stick. But it had been following him from the sports centre on Melrose Road. So why couldn't he see anybody?

'Hey, you! Show yourself!'

No answer. But the tapping stopped.

1   How does the writer's use of language capture the tense nature of the incident?   **4**

2   What view of Harry's character are we offered through the writer's use of language as the boy tries to work out the source of the noise?   **4**

THINGS TO DO AND THINK ABOUT

As we said at the beginning of this section, these are practice questions to help you with what to say about **sentence structure**. The words 'writer's language' in an exam should, of course, alert you to the fact that you are being invited to analyse **other** language techniques as well.

Look at all three extracts again, and this time answer the questions with reference to word choice and imagery.

 DON'T FORGET

If you're struggling to identify any striking pieces of imagery or word choice to analyse in your exam paper, look for interesting use of sentence structure and punctuation!

 ONLINE TEST

Head to www.brightredbooks.net and take the test on this section.

 ONLINE

Learn more about punctuation by reading the guide at www.brightredbooks.net

TONE

Candidates often find questions on tone challenging. This is understandable: it's not as easy to identify tone in a written text as it is in conversation. You need to learn to spot tone markers or context clues – and, as with punctuation marks and sentence types, once you know what you're looking for, you can memorise them and have them at your fingertips in the exam.

HOW TO IDENTIFY TONE

Here are some of the major tone markers. Once you know and recognise them, they will help you to determine the overall tone of the passage. After you've done that, you'll need to find specific examples from the text to support your answer.

TONE	MARKERS	INTENDED EFFECT
Chatty/informal/ colloquial	Short sentences Abbreviations: *can't, it'll, won't* Free use of first/second-person pronouns: *I, you* Chatty expressions: *Come on! Right on! No problem.* Free use of exclamation and question marks. Sentences without a verb. (Minor sentences.) *No change there then.* Slang expressions: *Back in a jiffy, a smack on the gob* Informal commands: *Go early ... Take a picnic ... Stay away from ...*	To get persuasively closer to the reader, giving the effect of someone chatting informally to his/her friends.
Humorous	Use of exaggeration or a series of exaggerations (also called hyperbole): *He was so thin I've seen more fat on a chip!* Telling jokes/stories against the speaker or topic. Mixing formal and informal styles: *Please refrain from asking for credit as a smack on the gob frequently offends.*	To strive for comic effect, sometimes simply to amuse, but sometimes to underline and mock the absurd/pointless nature of some issue under discussion.
Emotive	Use of words or phrases which stir up strong emotions: *weary pensioner, helpless infant, heartless thieves, terrified for their lives* Repetition of such words/phrases to intensify their effect: *weary of ..., weary of ... and weary of ...*	To arouse extremes of feeling in the face of fear, anger, suffering, injustice, loneliness or cruelty.
Ironic/tongue-in-cheek	Often saying the opposite of what you mean: *The concert lasts four hours? With no interval? How lovely!*	To criticise or mock something or somebody in a humorous way to make a critical point.

contd

Persuasive	Using comparatives/superlatives: *A better way of banking, the best in its class, the newest sat-nav* Words highlighting excellence: *quality, perfection, integrity* Words suggesting trustworthiness: *for generations, the choice of experts* Rhetorical questions: *What kind of parent sends a child to school hungry?*	To win over readers to the author's point of view/beliefs.
Factual/matter-of-fact	Usually created by a series of statements which avoid any of the above slanting of information: *Comets are more common than is popularly imagined. Astronomers believe that as many as one trillion could exist in the farther reaches of the solar system. Best known of all is Halley's Comet.*	To impart information in a neutral, unemotional manner. Sometimes used effectively to contrast with the more colourful tones described above. Facts and statistics may appear.

 THINGS TO DO AND THINK ABOUT

Here are five different extracts. Identify the tone used in each of them. Which tone markers helped you to arrive at your answers?

1

'We believe in a generous America, in a compassionate America, in a tolerant America open to the dreams of an immigrant's daughter who studies in our schools and pledges to our flag, to the young boy on the south side of Chicago who sees a life beyond the nearest street corner, to the furniture worker's child in North Carolina who wants to become a doctor or a scientist, an engineer or an entrepreneur, a diplomat or even a president.'

(President Barack Obama, election-night victory speech, 7 November 2012)

2

It has been one of the finest summers our family can remember: the basement flooded no less than three times; Jake caught pneumonia on his beach holiday and Alice came back from holiday to find herself unemployed. A great season all round, I'd say. One of the very best.

3

For generations, our whisky has stood the test of time for quality. According to world experts, it is not just the finest in its class, but the touchstone of excellence for the entire industry, a beacon of perfection in a mediocre world. What other choice is there when only the best will do?

4

So, you with me? Up for making your parents proud? I thought so. Here's how we'll do it. Turn to page 14. Read what it says about positive thinking. Go on, do it now. Did that ring a bell with you? I thought so. Who wouldn't want that sweet smell of success? That seal of approval from all your family? All this could be yours. How so? Just fill in this coupon, send £15.50 and our guide will be winging its way to you, lickety-split.

5

The number of people playing sport at least once a week is higher than at any time before the Olympic Games and, at 15.5 million, is 100,000 higher than it was in April 2012. Sport England and the government highlight the fact that 1.5 million more adults are playing sport regularly than when the bid for the Olympics was won in 2005.

 DON'T FORGET

Always be alert to the fact that writers can employ a variety of tones in a passage. They might begin in one tone and end in another, or they might combine two tones at once – for example, humorous and colloquial.

If the question on tone appears to be a high-value one, make sure that you provide plenty of evidence. One example is not enough. Make sure your evidence is sufficiently substantial to pick up maximum marks.

 ONLINE TEST

Want to revise your knowledge of this? Head to www.brightredbooks.net and take the test.

ONLINE

Head to www.brightredbooks.net and follow the link 'Tones' for a long list of different tones used in language analysis.

EVALUATING 1

In the evaluation question, you are being asked to assess how successfully a particular section of the passage achieves a particular effect. The wording might vary, but basically you are being asked to **evaluate the effectiveness** of a particular section of the text, or to say **how well** or **how effectively** you believe the writer has expressed or conveyed a certain idea to the audience.

EVALUATING YOUR ANALYSIS

If you're worried about repeating comments that you've made in an analysis answer, don't be. You need to analyse first before you can evaluate. The difference is that you have to take this analysis a good bit further. As well as saying **how** the writer has used language, you need to give your own opinion about **how well** or **successfully** the writer has used that language to achieve their objective.

You will be asked to evaluate the effectiveness of one or more of the following:

- a particular language technique (for example, figurative language and sentence structure)
- an anecdote, illustration or example
- the conclusion.

When you are answering an evaluation question, take the usual three-stage approach first:

1 Locate specific items from the text (unless the question has already done so).

2 Identify a language technique that the writer is using (unless the question has already done so).

3 Explain in your own words the effect that this technique has on the reader.

Then take it one stage further:

4 Give a personal assessment, backed up by textual evidence, of how successful you find this technique to be.

DON'T FORGET

Evaluation questions ask for **your** opinion about how well or otherwise you think the writer has conveyed an idea to readers. You need to have confidence in your own knowledge and ideas.

DON'T FORGET

Usually, the writing you are being asked to comment on has been chosen for its excellence in the eyes of the person setting the paper. If, however, you wish to make a negative evaluative comment on some point, you are perfectly at liberty to do so. But be very careful. You will need to back up your comment with convincing evidence from the text and a soundly argued case. An exam is no place to air private prejudices.

EVALUATING A TECHNIQUE

Here is an extract that you're familiar with (see page 15). You've already read it and answered questions (1) and (2). We've now added (3), an evaluation question on page 25.

> Nothing is more stimulating, on a gleaming spring day, than the kaleidoscopic Basin of St Mark, the pool that lies directly before the Piazzetta. In the day-time the basin is never calm, however still the weather, because of the constant churning of ships and propellers: but at night, if you take your boat out there through the lamplight, it is as still and dark and luscious as a great lake of plum-juice, through which your bows seep thickly, and into whose sickly viscous liquid the dim shape of the Doge's Palace seems to be slowly sinking, like a pastry pavilion.

(From Jan Morris, *Venice*, Faber and Faber, London, 1993)

contd

3   Explain how effective you find the writer's language in capturing the night-time character of the Basin.   **3**

So, how do we start? The best approach to tackling question (3) is probably to look back at how you answered question (1). Here's an example of a candidate's response to question (1):

> 'luscious': this word choice is particularly effective in conveying the texture of the Basin's water at night since it is usually associated with fruit, not water, and the reader is reminded of the thick juiciness of the mentioned plum-juice, suggesting also by its onomatopoeia the dense smoothness of the water.
>
> 'as a great lake of plum-juice': this simile is effective both in suggesting the dark, purplish colour of the water and suggesting a texture which seems much thicker than might be expected of water. It is also startling in suggesting that this plum-juice is covering an area far beyond what we might normally expect such a liquid to cover.

This candidate has explained very thoroughly how the writer's word choice and imagery work on the reader. But they haven't yet answered **how effective** they think these language techniques are. They do so very effectively in their response to question (3) below:

> The writer's word choice of 'luscious' and the simile 'as a great lake of plum-juice' **are effective in contributing to a view** of the night-time seascape which is startlingly original in the way it avoids the clichés of more conventional descriptions of water. By employing terms which are more often associated with fruit ('luscious') and fruit drinks ('plum-juice'), she uses our familiarity with their thicker textures to make us use our sense of taste, texture and colour to recreate in our own minds how the night-time water appeared to her. In saying it was a 'great lake of plum-juice', she again catches not only the colour and texture but also extent of the waterscape before her. **These examples of word choice and imagery are, in their marked originality, highly successful in capturing a very particular and persuasive image of the Basin at night.**

 THINGS TO DO AND THINK ABOUT

Don't worry about repeating comments you've made in your analysis answer – you're bound to do this to some extent because evaluation naturally follows on from analysis. Remember, however, that the examiner is looking for an evaluation answer that will take this analysis a good bit further. Always include your own opinion of how well you think the overall objective of the writer's intentions is being met by specified items of language.

 ONLINE TEST

How well have you learned this topic? Take the test at www.brightredbooks.net

VIDEO LINK

For some great examples of language analysis, head to www.brightredbooks.net

EVALUATING 2

EVALUATING AN ANECDOTE/ILLUSTRATION/EXAMPLE

Here's another extract that you've familiar with and have answered analysis questions on (see page 15). As in the previous section, we've added an evaluation question for you to try.

> The most fetching book I've come across for ages wasn't in a traditional bookshop but on a recent visit to the South London Gallery in Peckham. It was Thackeray's *Vanity Fair*, but not the Penguin Popular Classic. This one was pale pink and as big as a box, newly typeset, accompanied by 30 gorgeous illustrations. So, even as the big beasts of publishing struggle, and their traditional retailers lurch from crisis to crisis, there are reasons to be hopeful. Some publishers are doing well by producing objects beautiful enough to be collectible. That *Vanity Fair* I saw is from Four Corners Books, a tiny east London publisher with two employees; as well as new books, Four Corners knocks out "Familiars" by inviting contemporary artists to create fresh editions of classic novels and short stories.

(From James Harkin, 'A whole new e-chapter', in the *Guardian*, 26 April 2011)

Let's add evaluation question (4) to the three analysis questions you have already answered in the earlier section.

4   In the context of changing habits in publishing, how effective do you find the writer's anecdote about the edition of *Vanity Fair* that he discovered recently?   **4**

Here's an example of a candidate's response to question (4):

> Given that the essence of the article is about the changing face of publishing, the fact that this edition was, unusually, in pink, the size of a box and elaborately illustrated **brings home vividly to the reader** the extent of the changes which are already happening in book production. The fact that it was found, not in a traditional bookshop, but in an art gallery, suggests also that not only is the appearance of books changing but also the location in which we might expect to find them. **These changes which are described in this graphic anecdote launch effectively** the main thrust of this article dealing with the changing world of publishing.

EVALUATING A CONCLUSION

Here, the examiner wants to know how successfully **you think** the concluding paragraph rounds off the passage for the reader.

Sometimes, the wording of the question will point you towards a particular aspect such as tone. Sometimes, you're left to consider the effectiveness or appropriateness of the conclusion in your own terms. Where this is the case, you need to decide what **you** feel is a satisfactory way to conclude the passage.

contd

WHAT MAKES AN EFFECTIVE CONCLUSION?

Does it revisit the passage's main points?	Often, writers in this kind of passage like to remind us of the various strands explored in the passage as a whole. In this way, the reader is left considering the key points made earlier. By summarising them in the final lines, the writer clarifies and intensifies his/her arguments.	In referring again to ..., ... and ..., the writer is pulling together facts mentioned earlier and so clarifies and intensifies his/her arguments. In so doing, the writer provides an effective sense of completion to the passage.
Does it connect with the opening?	Writers like to present readers with a well-shaped article. One way to impose form is to connect in some way with the opening lines. Was there a question in the introduction which is now conclusively answered here? Was there an image invoked at the start which is referred to again here – for example, a door that was opened has now closed? Was an image used which is developed again in some way? This circularity of approach is a popular one. Part of your answer could deal with this. But don't stop there: keep looking for other connecting features.	In the introduction, the writer asked if ... In the conclusion, the writer sums up his/her answer, which has been built up over the course of the article. In so doing, the writer provides an effective sense of completion to the question posed. In the introduction, the writer uses the image of a door opening onto a new experience. In the conclusion, he mentions closing that door, bringing a sense of finality to the article's examination of ... In so doing, the writer provides an effective sense of completion to the passage.
Does it revisit and connect?	Often, journalists will adopt both techniques. Make sure to check for the existence of both if you wish to pick up full marks in this often high-value question.	

There are many other ways of concluding an article. Here are some examples:

- Does the writer call for action to deal with the topic under consideration? In that case, has he/she provided sufficient evidence (facts, statistics) to make action credible or worthwhile?

- Does the writer end with a warning? If so, has he/she made a sufficiently worrying case (anecdotes, statistics) for us to take on board these concerns?

- Does the writer universalise his/her own personal experience? If this is the case, are his/her attempts convincing? Has the case been made persuasively enough (anecdotes, examples, imagery) for us to share this experience?

- Does the writer perhaps change tone here? What is the change? For apparently what purpose? Do you find the change effective in completing the piece?

 ## THINGS TO DO AND THINK ABOUT

Good writers will always surprise us with their approaches to rounding off a passage. **Analyse** carefully what is happening in the last paragraph and be prepared to **point to features** the writer has presented there. Then **evaluate** in your own terms how successful you feel the writer has been.

 ONLINE TEST

Head to www.brightredbooks.net and take the test on this section.

 ONLINE

Read more about effective conclusions at www.brightredbooks.net

LET'S TRY OUT WHAT WE HAVE LEARNED 1

So far in this chapter, you have examined the types of questions you should expect in the Reading for Understanding, Analysis and Evaluation exam, and the techniques you need to answer them successfully. Now, let's put these elements together in the format in which you will meet them in the exam.

Over the following pages, there are two passages – passage A and passage B – that examine happiness in the Nordic countries, with the focus largely on Denmark. Read both passages and then attempt the six questions that follow passage B.

The final question for this passage asks you to summarise certain points. Go back to what we said about summarising on page 9 before you tackle this question.

DON'T FORGET

Before you launch into answering a question, always check first that you're not in danger of galloping ahead and writing information that you'll need to use to answer the next one. Each question will be looking for different things.

DON'T FORGET

Always check the number of marks being allocated for a question. This will help you determine how much time you should be spending on it.

PASSAGE A

For the past few years the world has been in thrall to all things Nordic. "The Sweet Danish Life: Copenhagen: Cool, Creative, Carefree," simpered *National Geographic*; "The Nordic Countries: The Next Supermodel", boomed the *Economist*; "Copenhagen really is wonderful for so many reasons," gushed the Guardian.

I have contributed to the relentless shower of print columns on the wonders of Scandinavia myself over the years but now I say: enough! *Nu er det nok!* Enough with foraging for dinner. Enough with the impractical minimalist interiors. Enough with the envious reports on the abolition of gender-specific pronouns. Enough of the unblinking idolatry of all things knitted, bearded, rye bread-based and licorice-laced. It is time to redress the imbalance, shed a little light Beyond the Wall.

Take the Danes, for instance. True, they claim to be the happiest people in the world, but why no mention of the fact they are second only to Iceland when it comes to consuming anti-depressants?

Actually, I have lived in Denmark – on and off – for about a decade, because my wife's work is here (and she's Danish). Life here is pretty comfortable, more so for indigenous families than for immigrants or ambitious go-getters, but as with all the Nordic nations, it remains largely free of armed conflict, extreme poverty, natural disasters and Jeremy Kyle.

So let's remove those rose-tinted ski goggles and take a closer look at the objects of our infatuation …

Why do the Danes score so highly on international happiness surveys? Well, they do have high levels of trust and social cohesion, and do very nicely from industrial pork products, but according to the OECD they also work fewer hours per year than most of the rest of the world. As a result, productivity is worryingly sluggish. How can they afford all those expensively foraged meals and hand-knitted woollens? Simple, the Danes also have the highest level of private debt in the world (four times as much as the Italians, to put it into context; enough to warrant a warning from the IMF), while more than half of them admit to using the black market to obtain goods and services.

contd

Perhaps the Danes' dirtiest secret is that, according to a 2012 report from the Worldwide Fund for Nature, they have the fourth largest per capita ecological footprint in the world. Even ahead of the US. Those offshore windmills may look impressive as you land at Kastrup, but Denmark burns an awful lot of coal. Worth bearing that in mind the next time a Dane wags her finger at your patio heater.

Presumably the correlative of this is that Denmark has the best public services? According to the OECD's Programme for International Student Assessment rankings (Pisa), Denmark's schools lag behind even the UK's. Its health service is buckling too. (The other day, I turned up at my local A&E to be told that I had to make an appointment, which I can't help feeling rather misunderstands the nature of the service.) According to the World Cancer Research Fund, the Danes have the highest cancer rates on the planet.

Most seriously of all, economic equality – which many believe is the foundation of societal success – is decreasing. According to a report in *Politiken* this month, the proportion of people below the poverty line has doubled over the last decade. Denmark's provinces have become a social dumping ground for non-western immigrants, the elderly, the unemployed and the unemployable who live alongside Denmark's 22m intensively farmed pigs, raised 10 to a pen and pumped full of antibiotics (the pigs, that is).

Other awkward truths? There is more than a whiff of the police state about the fact that Danish policemen refuse to display ID numbers and can refuse to give their names. Like the Swedes, they embraced privatisation with great enthusiasm (even the ambulance service is privatised) and can seem spectacularly unsophisticated in their race relations (cartoon depictions of black people with big lips and bones through their noses are not uncommon in the national press). And if you think a move across the North Sea would help you escape the paedophiles, racists, crooks and tax-dodging corporations one reads about in the British media on a daily basis, I'm afraid I must disabuse you of that too. Got plenty of them.

Plus side? No one talks about cricket.

(Abridged from Michael Booth, 'Dark lands: the grim truth behind the "Scandinavian miracle"', in the *Guardian*, 27 January 2014)

LET'S TRY OUT WHAT WE HAVE LEARNED 2

PASSAGE B

Last month, Denmark was crowned the happiest country in the world. "The top countries generally rank higher in all six of the key factors identified in the World Happiness Report," wrote University of British Columbia economics professor John Helliwell, one of the report's contributing authors. "Together, these six factors explain three quarters of differences in life evaluations across hundreds of countries and over the years."

The six factors for a happy nation split evenly between concerns on a government- and on a human-scale. The happiest countries have in common a large GDP per capita, healthy life expectancy at birth and a lack of corruption in leadership. But also essential were three things over which individual citizens have a bit more control: a sense of social support, freedom to make life choices and a culture of generosity.

"There is now a rising worldwide demand that policy be more closely aligned with what really matters to people as they themselves characterize their well-being," economist Jeffrey Sachs said in a statement at the time of the report's release.

But why Denmark over any of the other wealthy, democratic countries with small, educated populations? And can the qualities that make this Nordic country the happiest around apply to other cultures across the globe? Here are a few things Danes do well that any of us can lobby for. […]

Danish children have access to free or low-cost child care. And early childhood education is associated with health and well-being throughout life for its recipients – as well as for mothers. What's more, this frees up young mothers to return to the work force if they'd like to. The result? In Denmark, 79 percent of mothers return to their previous level of employment, compared to 59 percent of American women. These resources mean that women contribute 34 to 38 percent of income in Danish households with children, compared to American women, who contribute 28 percent of income.

Danish citizens expect and receive health care as a basic right. But what's more, they know how to effectively use their health systems. Danish people are in touch with their primary care physician an average of nearly seven times per year, according to a 2012 survey of family medicine in the country. And that means they have a single advocate who helps them navigate more complicated care.

"This gatekeeping system essentially is designed to support the principle that treatment ought to take place at the lowest effective care level along with the idea of continuity of care provided by a family doctor," wrote the authors of the family medicine survey.

(Abridged from 'Denmark is the Happiest Country. You'll Never Guess Why', in the *Huffington Post*, 23 October 2013)

QUESTIONS

Questions on Passage A

1   Re-read the first paragraph.

   a   Identify two press opinions on the Nordic countries noted recently by the writer. **2**

   b   Analyse how the writer's use of language in paragraph 1 emphasises his distaste for these opinions. You should refer in your answer to such features as sentence structure, word choice, imagery, contrast and tone. **4**

2   Re-read the second paragraph.

   a   Identify two issues which he finds unattractive about Nordic lifestyles. **2**

   b   By referring to at least two features of language in this paragraph, analyse how the writer conveys the strength of his feelings towards Nordic lifestyles. You should refer in your answer to such features as sentence structure, word choice, imagery, contrast, tone ... **4**

3   Re-read paragraph four.

   a   Identify any two reasons why the writer seems to respect Denmark. **2**

   b   By referring to at least two features of language, analyse how the writer seeks to win our approval for Denmark. You should refer in your answer to such features as sentence structure, word choice, imagery, contrast and tone. **4**

4   a   'Why do the Danes score so highly on international happiness surveys?' the writer asks in paragraph 6. According to the writer, in what ways does he find them in paragraph 6 lacking in a real basis for satisfaction with their lot? **4**

   b   By referring to two examples of the writer's use of language in paragraphs 6 and 7, analyse how he seeks to convince us of his viewpoint. You should refer in your answer to such features as sentence structure, word choice, imagery, contrast and tone. **4**

5   Re-read the final paragraph.

   a   By referring to at least one example of the writer's use of tone, analyse how he seeks to sway our opinion of Denmark. **4**

   b   Evaluate the final paragraph's effectiveness as a conclusion to the passage as a whole. **2**

Question on Passage A and B

6   Both writers examine the Danish lifestyle. Identify key areas on which they disagree. In your answer, you should refer in detail to both passages. You may answer this question in continuous prose or in a series of bullet points. **5**

ONLINE

For the answers to these questions, head to www.brightredbooks.net/ subjects/higherenglish/ c02_08

 THINGS TO DO AND THINK ABOUT

Go over your answers carefully before you check them. Have you used your own words when asked to 'identify' or 'explain'? In questions which ask you to 'analyse', have you offered specific items of language, named them and explained their effect on the reader? And in questions which ask you to 'evaluate', have you analysed how the language techniques work and said how well you think they convey what the writer intended? At this practice stage, it's more important to go about answering the questions in the right way than getting them all correct.

SCOTTISH LITERATURE IN HIGHER

Over the centuries, Scotland has produced a canon of literature that is universally regarded as one of the richest in Western civilisation. National 5 English and the new CfE Higher English recognise this fully and are helping students to begin to explore it. For Higher, the choices for prose, poetry and drama cover a wide choice of styles and periods:

ONLINE

Look at our online suggestions at www.brightredbooks.net to find out more about some of these texts and the resources that are available to support you as you study them.

THE CHOICES

DRAMA	PROSE	POETRY
The Cheviot, the Stag and the Black, Black Oil by John McGrath	*Short stories* (a selection) by Iain Crichton Smith	Carol Ann Duffy
Men Should Weep by Ena Lamont Stewart	*Short stories* (a selection) by George Mackay Brown	Robert Burns
The Slab Boys by John Byrne	*Sunset Song* by Lewis Grassic Gibbon	Don Paterson
	The Cone-Gatherers by Robin Jenkins	Liz Lochhead
	The Trick is to Keep Breathing by Janice Galloway	Sorley MacLean
		Norman MacCaig

Those of you who are progressing to the CfE Higher from National 5 will be well aware of the important role that Scottish literature plays in this exam. The critical reading of a Scottish text (or texts) in Section 1 of the English Critical Reading paper counts for 20 marks in the overall exam total of 70 marks. 10 marks will be awarded for answering specific questions on a selected passage. A further 10 marks (usually in the final question) will be awarded for making links to other poems, plays or prose works by the same author, or for making links to other related sections within your chosen poem, play or prose work.

Whichever text you and your teacher have chosen to study, you'll have to know it inside out, because you never know which part of the text the examiners will select for comment. If you haven't got in-depth textual knowledge, you won't be able to comment authoritatively on the language, or relate the extract to similar or contrasting concepts and techniques elsewhere within the same text or in the author's other works.

Over the next few pages, we will analyse one example from each of the possible prose, drama or poetry selections. This will help you in two ways. If you have chosen these particular texts, the commentaries will supplement your existing notes and will help you to get to know them in greater detail. But perhaps even more usefully, our analyses will help you to become familiar both with the critical vocabulary and terminology you are expected to use, and with the kind of questions you will be asked and the type of answers you will be expected to give.

SO, WHAT'S NEW?

The demands outlined above will be familiar to N5 candidates. So, what has changed for Higher? While there is a slight change in the balance of marks between the two sections, the real difference is in the course's name: Higher. You will need to demonstrate a greater maturity of approach to the analytical process: the points you make should reveal a greater depth of insight than you may have shown in earlier exams; your expression will need to be similarly more polished and persuasive. But don't be alarmed: the preparation you have already done for National 5, together with this year's Higher course study, will stand you in good stead for the increased demands.

And this guide is specifically structured to help boost your confidence and competence in the face of these challenges.

THINGS TO DO AND THINK ABOUT

Even if your school or college supplies you with the text(s) you are studying, consider getting your own copy early on in the course. (You can usually buy a cheap second-hand copy online.) Mark up key passages of **your own copy** with a highlighter and add your teacher's and your own comments in the margins. This will help you to remember vital information when you come to revise.

ONLINE

Check out the multiple facets of Scottish literature. Go to '100 Best Scottish Books' at www.brightredbooks.net, where you'll find some of the set prose works discussed by established authors.

ONLINE

For a rich source of background information and resource materials on Scottish literature, check out the Association for Scottish Literary Studies via www.brightredbooks.net

DON'T FORGET

Even if you are not studying the specific texts analysed in this section, you will be able to transfer what you have learned about technique to your own Scottish text, and apply this in the exam.

DON'T FORGET

What you have already learned about discussing Scottish literature for National 5 forms a sound basis for progressing on to Higher English. What you need to do now is to add depth and detail to your comments and greater fluency to your expression.

ONLINE TEST

How well have you learned this topic? Take the test at www.brightredbooks.net

THE INITIAL QUESTIONS: SKILLS REQUIRED

If you have sat National 5 English, then you'll already be familiar with answering questions on set Scottish texts in Section 1 of the Critical Reading paper. Remember that in Critical Reading you are being tested on your ability to understand, analyse and evaluate your chosen text. The initial questions will probably focus on the following key areas:

FIGURATIVE LANGUAGE

Here, your knowledge of metaphors, similes, personification, alliteration, onomatopoeia and so on from Reading for Understanding, Analysis and Evaluation will help you to identify the devices that the writer is using, and the effect they have on the reader. For Higher, you need to go into considerable depth about this. Look back at page 14 to remind yourself about these devices and how authors use them.

WORD CHOICE

It's essential that you are able to spot how a writer uses a particular word in an interesting way, and comment in depth on its connotations. You need to analyse and evaluate how successfully authors influence their readers by their choice of one word rather than another. Look back at page 12 to remind yourself about word choice.

SENTENCE STRUCTURE

Writers use sentence structure (and punctuation) to affect and influence their readers' response. Remind yourself about these devices by looking back at page 16.

ONLINE

Head to the Digital Zone and follow the 'Hazard Perception Game' link to test out your knowledge of language techniques!

TONE

Refresh your knowledge of the devices that writers use to convey tone or mood by looking back at page 22.

THE WORDING OF QUESTIONS

Pay close attention to the wording of the question to ensure that you are giving the examiners exactly what they want.

Sometimes the question will test your detailed **understanding** of what is happening in an extract. The clue is in the wording:

> **By referring closely to ...** explain what **is revealed about ...**
>
> **With close reference to the text,** discuss the attitudes **of ...**

You will need to identify words or phrases and then say what they tell us about the person, thing, situation, or whatever the examiner is asking.

> 'ran ... hacked down ... charged in' tells us the boy was energetic, with perhaps a hint of violence about him.

contd

Sometimes you will be asked to demonstrate your **analytical** skills. Again, the clue is in the wording:

> Analyse how **in lines 10–15 the writer conveys a sense of ***'s growing confidence in her future.**
>
> **By referring closely to two examples of ******'s speech,** explain how ...

When you answer questions of this type, pick out specific words/ phrases/techniques, unpack them fully and explain clearly the effect that they have on the reader.

'I can + verb': repetition of parallel structures with regard to her future plans (clean, strip and wash, open, paint, lift). All references here are to fixing up or getting into order her surroundings, until now neglected, hinting at a more positive view of her future.

The question might also ask you to make your own assessment or **evaluation** of some aspect of the extract:

> Evaluate the effectiveness **of lines 1–4 as an opening to ...**
>
> How effective **do you find the speech of ...?**

For these types of questions, you will need to identify what is happening in the featured lines, analyse how the writer has used specific words or phrases to achieve a particular effect and then assess how well you think they have succeeded. Remember – it's your opinion that the examiner is looking for here.

The poem is about a descent from early success to disorder, often dealing humorously with this descent: from the top, then, the zenith: suggests that we are starting at the height of their career and already that the movement is from that.

majestic in ankle-length shorts: the ludicrous image of shorts reaching down to the ankles sets up a humorous tone right from the start.

 THINGS TO DO AND THINK ABOUT

By this point, you've probably realised that most of what you have learned in the Reading for Understanding, Analysis and Evaluation chapter will also help you to tackle questions on the Scottish texts. Re-read the chapter to familiarise yourself with the various devices and techniques and their effect on the reader.

 DON'T FORGET

Always check out the value of questions before you start to write anything. If a question is worth 4 marks, then make sure that your answer gives two full comments and two examples of whatever is required.

 ONLINE TEST

Head to www.brightredbooks.net and take the test on this section.

THE FINAL QUESTION: SKILLS REQUIRED

The final question in Section 1 of the Critical Reading paper is the high-value one worth 10 marks. To answer this question, you need to make links to other parts of your text or to other works the author has written, so you need to have in-depth knowledge of that text.

We'll look at the final question for poetry, prose and drama in turn.

ONLINE

For those studying poetry texts, go to the home page of the Scottish Poetry Library at www.scottishpoetrylibrary.org.uk and key in 'Don Paterson', 'Robert Burns', 'Liz Lochhead' or 'Sorley MacLean'. Here you will find full biographical notes, some of the poems listed for study and lots of advice for further reading. You can also ask the staff for more detailed information. This is an invaluable website for CfE Higher English students. Don Paterson and Carol Ann Duffy also have useful websites of their own.

POETRY

Here, the final question will invite you to make connections between ideas and/or language that you have noticed both in this poem and in at least one other poem by the same author. For example, the poet might portray a character in another poem who thinks, reacts or relates to others in the same way as a character in the poem you are studying. Or there could be aspects of relationships that crop up more than once.

In terms of language, does the poet use a recurring style feature such as a conversational tone with enjambment? Is the poem rich in other poetic devices, or is it deliberately matter-of-fact, using everyday language? Does the poet appear in the poem, or is somebody else narrating the poem? Does the poet always write in free verse, or sometimes use a specific form? Is the poem written in Scots or English? You need to be able to make connections at several possible levels between the ideas and language of the poem in the exam paper and at least one other poem you have studied.

PROSE

If you have been reading one of the selections of short stories, then a lot of what we've said about poetry will also apply here. Check if there are certain similar or contrasting ideas, situations or characters in the extract that link to at least one of the five other stories of your choice. For example, is there lack of communication between the generations, or scenes in which characters confront or misunderstand each other?

If you are studying a novel, then look for other incidents in the novel where, for example, a character shows similar or contrasting behaviour, or where they show developing understanding or emotional depth. What has caused this change? Perhaps one character is viewed in several ways by others in the novel? Maybe a theme is revisited in a way which parallels or contrasts with its treatment elsewhere in the novel? Are there other scenes where setting or atmosphere seems particularly important? What does setting contribute to the overall effect of the incident on the reader? Has setting been used this way before?

DRAMA

Many of the points about variations in character, theme and setting discussed above also apply to a passage taken from a play.

With a play, however, the action unrolls via dialogue, which needs to be carefully examined for typical speech characteristics. Do some characters have topics to which they regularly return? Do characters typically appear to ask questions, give instructions, sound optimistic or pessimistic, talk about trivia, act violently, need help or say too little or too much? How well do characters listen to each other? Are there moments when this changes? What is the effect of this change on us, the audience?

Are there stage props that take on symbolic meanings in different parts of the play? Does lighting change at any key points? And what is the effect of this? Do stage directions differ here from an earlier episode? Do the costumes of the characters change at any point? What do the changes tell us?

 THINGS TO DO AND THINK ABOUT

Don't leave revising your knowledge of links until the last minute. Get together regularly with a friend or someone in your class, and look for links between two stories or two poems, or between two characters as they appear at various stages in a novel or play. Note down your ideas and add them to your revision notes.

 DON'T FORGET

Having your own copy of a text is always a good idea because you can use it to make notes in the margin about parallels, links, similarities or contrasts. If you also add in page references, it will save you lots of time when you come to revise.

 ONLINE TEST

How well have you learned this topic? Take the test at www.brightredbooks.net

JOHN McGRATH: *THE CHEVIOT, THE STAG AND THE BLACK, BLACK OIL*

JOHN McGRATH: AN INTRODUCTION

Born in 1935 into an Irish Catholic family in Birkenhead, John McGrath gained fame as a prolific writer and passionately committed man of the theatre. As founder/director of the 7:84 Theatre Company, he believed that the function of theatre was to reach out to people who had no history of theatre-going. As he saw it, theatre existed not only to entertain the public but also to encourage them to consider those social issues affecting them in their daily lives. By so doing, he hoped to help them bring about changes for the better in their society.

In addition to writing over seventy plays, he also worked as a writer and director of films and popular television programmes. He received Lifetime Achievement Awards from both BAFTA (in 1993) and the Writers' Guild of Great Britain (in 1997), as well as honorary doctorates from the University of Stirling and the University of London. He died in 2002.

THE PLAY'S BACKGROUND

You ask me if the play has any overt political intention. We certainly are not proselytising for any party or group, openly or secretly. The play is intended, as all our work is, to help people to a greater awareness of their situation and their potential: how they achieve that potential is their affair not ours. So have no fears, we shan't be canvassing for anybody, merely fulfilling one of the oldest functions of the theatre (cf. Euripides, Aristophanes et al.)

(Quoted by his wife Elizabeth MacLennan in *The Moon Belongs to Everyone,* London, Methuen, 1990)

Written in 1973, *The Cheviot, the Stag and the Black, Black Oil* is McGrath's most famous play, highlighting the harsh realities of life of working-class Scots from the early nineteenth-century Clearances until the 1970s. In McGrath's hands, what might have been wearisome political propaganda emerges as a hugely energetic theatre piece, persuasive in its inventiveness. Yet his political engagement could cause him problems. Here's his answer to an earlier query from the Drama Director of the Scottish Arts Council (from whom he hoped to receive backing for his play) in February 1973:

In denying any 'political intention', McGrath is perhaps being a little disingenuous. True, the play is critical of both Nationalist and Labour parties, but the title of the play's performing company – the 7:84 – stems from a 1966 article in *The Economist* which revealed that 7 per cent of the nation's citizens owned 84 per cent of the nation's wealth. This imbalance was one that McGrath felt keenly throughout his career; and *The Cheviot, the Stag and the Black, Black Oil* is a highly critical, though hugely entertaining, scrutiny of this imbalance through the medium of a set of music-hall sketches, folk songs, eye-witness accounts, documentary material and audience participation, which came later to be known as a 'ceilidh-play'.

DON'T FORGET

Your own copy of this play will be useful for revision purposes. A second-hand copy will do, since you will probably want to make notes in the margin and highlight key quotations. You can then use these to revise at exam time.

THE CEILIDH-PLAY

Although it came to be known as a 'ceilidh' play, *The Cheviot, the Stag and the Black, Black Oil* has antecedents in both the drama of sixteenth-century Scotland and of early twentieth-century Germany.

Sir David Lindsay's *Ane Satyre of the Thrie Estaites* was concerned, like this play, with the governance of Scotland, as seen from various standpoints.

The German dramas of Berthold Brecht, as well as employing popular music and music-hall routines to examine political realities, revelled in the idea that the audience was fully aware they were watching a group of actors putting on a play, free from the mystique of the theatrical illusion, with each performer fully recognisable in various roles – as indeed they are here.

contd

First performed in March 1973 in Edinburgh, the play soon went on tour throughout the North and Highlands to much popular acclaim. Its form was thought to be highly original at the time. McGrath's wife, Elizabeth MacLennan, a fellow originator of and actor in the play, comments:

> The style was extraordinarily effective. It swung effortlessly from sadness to merriment.
>
> Nowadays, critics and academics refer confidently to 'the ceilidh-play', as though people had been writing them for years. But it was a new form. On the poster we called it 'a ceilidh play with scenes, songs and music of Highland history from the Clearances to the oil strike', but it was not a play in any accepted sense at that time. In the newspaper ads we called it 'a ceilidh entertainment with dance to follow'. [...] The set was a giant pop-up book, beautifully painted by John Byrne. It was perhaps the first touring show in which the actors changed in full view of the audience, and sat on the same level as the audience, only jumping on the rostra to act out episodes and songs. People found it fresh, strange, moving, exciting and very, very funny. They stayed behind to talk, argue, dance and enjoy themselves.

(Quoted by Elizabeth MacLennan in *The Moon Belongs to Everyone,* London, Methuen, 1990)

Although John McGrath had been mulling over the concept of this play for fifteen years, the actors and musicians of the 7:84 company were also drawn into its final format, sometimes checking areas of research, sometimes contributing jokes, ideas and musical possibilities. In other words, the involvement of all, which McGrath advocated for the future of Scotland, was also the guiding principle for the creation of the play itself.

THE STRUCTURE

It falls broadly into three time frames.

THE CHEVIOT

The *Cheviot* of the title deals with the Highland Clearances, which began in the second half of the eighteenth century. The effects of the Clearances are picked up in the play in early nineteenth-century Scotland. This was the time when hereditary aristocratic landowners discovered that they could make considerably more money from sheep than from crofters. Consequently, they enforced their tenants' eviction, often with great brutality, to make way for sheep enclosures.

John Byrne with his pop-up set for the play. Given that the whole troupe had to travel around the Highlands of Scotland in a Transit van and often perform within hours of arriving at a venue, a pop-up book offered the most time-saving (and space-saving) solution for a set.

THE STAG

The *Stag* of the title refers to the later nineteenth-century preoccupation of royalty, the aristocracy and rich industrialists with acquiring sporting estates for hunting deer and shooting grouse. The play focuses on the arrogant indifference with which they treated their estate workers and tenants.

THE BLACK, BLACK OIL

The *Black, Black Oil* is a reference to the discovery of oil in the North Sea and its exploitation from the mid-1960s onwards. Here, the butt of the satire is a combination of the greed of American oil companies and the ineptitude of British governments in dealing with them.

 ONLINE

Check out the National Library of Scotland's page about the play through www.brightredbooks.net

 THINGS TO DO AND THINK ABOUT

In 1974, John McGrath updated the stage play for a television version. Go to YouTube and key in the title of the play. Some of the material has been omitted or shortened, and the order has changed in places, but this 90-minute version conveys much of the spirit of the original play.

 ONLINE TEST

Head to www.brightredbooks.net and take the test on this section.

THE PLAY'S CHALLENGES

STRUCTURE

DON'T FORGET

Note that all page references are to the Methuen paperback edition of the play.

By this time, you'll have gathered that this play is clearly different from others you have studied. Given its episodic structure with sketches, folk songs, music-hall ditties, poems, eye-witness accounts and audience participation, it is a play in which you should not look for developed characterisation as in, for example, *Macbeth* or *The Crucible*. In place of acts and scenes and a gradually achieved dramatic climax, we are offered various forms of satirical comedy, political directness, emotional frankness – all geared for moment-to-moment effect. Members of the cast play multiple characters with minimal scenery, props and costumes, with no attempt to conceal the fact that they are actors acting parts rather than presenting a theatrical illusion of 'reality'. We, the audience, also find ourselves part of the production at times.

On first viewing this play, an audience might think it is a loose collection of entertaining items, interspersed with informal history lessons. On closer inspection, however, McGrath has maintained a sure hand in shaping its overall design to ensure its integrity as a unified theatre piece.

McGrath achieves this integrity through certain unifying **themes** which hold together the various proceedings on stage and by establishing certain recurring features of **structure and language.**

THEMES

THE CORROSIVE POWER OF CAPITAL

DON'T FORGET

Action (by the landowners) and reaction (by the people) are the life-blood of the play. If you know the forms that the exploitation took, the identity of the exploiters and the developing responses of the exploited, this will help you to link the exam passage to other passages in the play in the final Scottish Critical Reading question.

McGrath uses the destructive force of money as the major theme in the play's broad satirical sweep through two centuries of history. From the appointment of Patrick Sellar in 1809 as factor of the Sutherland estate to the coming of Texas Jim in the mid-1960s, the play exposes how capital is an ever-evolving, corrosive force in the lives of the people of the Highlands.

The first destabilisation came with the Clearances. Thanks to the expanding British Empire, land-rich aristocrats such as the Duke of Sutherland had steadily increasing capital that they were keen to invest. Agricultural economics of the time saw more profit in sheep than in people, and so the people found themselves evicted – some to the far-flung outposts of Empire (like Texas Jim's ancestor) and some to unprofitable fishing ventures along the coast. As we see from the play, many of these evictions were carried out with ruthless cruelty.

A second phase of destabilisation came with the decline of the profitability of sheep when the once-thriving wool trade collapsed in the late nineteenth century. Landowners now turned their land-holdings into sporting estates for the enjoyment of the likes of Lady Phosphate and Lord Crask, whose patronising indifference to the people who were still left on the land is satirised here. Those tenants who remained had little in the way of access to land or secure tenure.

The third phase of destabilisation began after the Second World War when the cash-strapped descendants of Lady Phosphate and Lord Crask again took to exploiting the land, this time in the guise of tourism. But now, people like Lord Vat of Glenlivet required the money of crass city property developers such as Andy McChuckemup to throw up shoddy tourist facilities. The aim was still the same: capital growth. Hard on the heels of tourism came the discovery of North Sea oil and the arrival of Texas Jim to exploit not only the resource itself but also the ineptitude of the British government.

contd

In this play, capital is seen as a destructive force that has led to the steady and painful depopulation of the Highlands, and to the steady erosion of Gaelic culture and language.

RESISTING CAPITAL FORCES

Just as the forms of exploitation evolve and develop over the time frame of the play, so, too, do the ways that the people respond to that exploitation.

The first eviction notices and the first responses we see date from 1813 at Strathnaver. There are three key points here: the conspicuous use of Gaelic, the lead role taken by strong-minded women and the conspicuous lack of organisation in this initial resistance.

In this early period, much of the violence is directed at soldiers, policemen and sheriff officers. It is reported as being led by women (pp. 11, 12 and 13) because many of the men are away in the Army 'defending the British way of life' (p. 45). But, we are told, '... for every township that fought back, there were many more who didn't'. Thanks to the Church's hostility to such action (pp. 12 and 13), these shows of resistance by the crofters, although feisty, are fairly isolated in their success. Why? For the moment, the fight-back lacks structured organisation, which seriously undermines the effective curbing of evictions.

A sign of change comes about in 1882 (p. 31) on the Glendale Estate. As the Younger Man points out, they have been unsuccessful so far in fighting back because 'we are divided among ourselves'. They pledge themselves to a rent strike; and, most significantly, the principle of organisation has now been established for the first time, with, however, varying degrees of success (pp. 31–37). Here we also notice the fact that Gaelic is less evident in the fight and that the struggle is now not simply to fight eviction but to raise (collectively) tenure grievances faced by the reduced numbers who have held on doggedly. Various Land Leagues are now set up to protect tenants' rights, and the government has established a Crofters' Commission to look into abuses. Tensions remain: landowners fail to respect new-won rights, and crofters retaliate with land-grabs (p. 53). For all their courageous efforts to organise, the Highlanders watch as their population, culture and language are slowly eroded throughout the late nineteenth century.

The only twentieth-century crofters we meet seem to have abandoned any semblance of resistance altogether, with the Wife and Crofter putting on a show of debased Highland culture and hospitality for the benefit of Rotherham tourists. They need to eke out a living now that the Crofter has been incapacitated by the oil industry. Their talk is of moving away to live in a flat, both adding sadly: 'We can't live here' (p. 72). The wheel has come full-circle for crofters. Despite the spirited fight to retain their place over all these decades, financial forces are evicting these twentieth-century crofters from their homes just as surely as Patrick Sellar evicted their ancestors.

But this is not the end for McGrath. For him the confrontation needs to be reinvigorated. He closes the play with a song – a Gaelic song – which enjoins the listeners (and presumably the audience, too) to fight on, suggesting his unshakeable belief in the power of culture and tradition to continue the struggle until:

> *Everyone in the land will have a place*
> *And the exploiter will be driven out.*

ONLINE

Key 'Community Buy-outs Scotland' into your browser and you will see that many of the changes proposed by the play have come about, not so much by 'the hardness of [...] fists' as by steady acquisitions by a variety of means. Find out what has happened to Glendale and Assynt and other places mentioned in the play.

THINGS TO DO AND THINK ABOUT

One way to add depth to your revision notes might be to list the contribution made by women to the central concerns of the play. Although no one woman is developed as a character, the women's presence at key moments in the play is well worth exploring. You should also note that the Gaelic Singer in the original production was a woman: Dolina MacLennan, a great Gaelic singer and actress.

ONLINE TEST

Want to revise your knowledge of this? Head to www.brightredbooks.net and take the test.

PRESENTATION OF THEMES

SATIRE AND PATHOS

When you analyse the text closely, you will see that McGrath maintains the audience's interest not only by the variety of action on the stage but also by switching the treatment of his themes between satire and pathos. These are useful terms for answering questions on this play, so let's look at their meaning.

SATIRE

This is when humour is used as a powerful criticism of some social abuse. The play is satirical in its overall stance, ridiculing constantly the greed underlying the exploitation of the Highlands and its resources by various groups. Landowners, judges, property developers, oil men and government ministers: all are targets for McGrath's satire, which employs a variety of tones from farce to irony.

PATHOS

This is a persuasive technique used to appeal to the audience's pity or compassion. It provides a powerful balance to the play's satire. We see this effectively at work in the play's Gaelic songs and poems. Their effect is strengthened when they are juxtaposed to incidents of particular cruelty or stupidity, highlighting in their quiet dignity the contrast between exploiter and exploited. We also observe pathos at work in many of the eye-witness accounts and statistics reported by the actors.

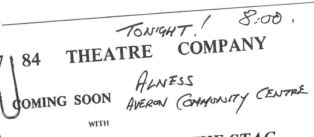

TONIGHT! 8:00,

7:84 THEATRE COMPANY

COMING SOON — ALNESS AVERON COMMUNITY CENTRE

WITH

THE CHEVIOT, THE STAG AND THE BLACK BLACK OIL.

PLAY / CEILIDH / DANCE / FIDDLER /
GAELIC SONGS / GIANT POP–UP BOOK /
FORCE TEN GAELS / OIL RIGS / TWO VANS /
PIPER / ELECTRIC PIANO / PENNY WHISTLE /
THE LOCH SEAFORTH / GUITARS / DRUMS /
SHEEP / DEER ....

A ONCE IN A LIFETIME CHANCE TO SEE:–
THE WOMEN OF COIGACH REPEL THE BAILLIFS
THE INDIANS MEET THE MEN OF THE HIGHLANDS ON THE RED RIVER
QUEEN VICTORIA SING AT THE CEILIDH
THE RETURN OF TEXAS JIM TO HIS GRANNIES HIELAN' HAME

WATCH OUT FOR POSTERS AND NEWSPAPERS

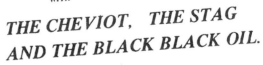

7% OF THE POPULATION OF THIS COUNTRY OWN 84% OF THE WEALTH.

STRUCTURE AND LANGUAGE

SONG AND PARODY

McGrath is alert to the usefulness of recurring songs and parodies of familiar songs – such as *These Are My Mountains* – as a shaping medium. The original, sung by all at the start of the play, establishes with the audience the driving idea behind McGrath's play: Scotland's land rightly belongs to Scotland's people. By having the audience join in so early on, McGrath is involving them, too, in the stewardship. The song is later, satirically, taken up by the sheep once **they** are in possession of the crofters' hillsides. A parody is sung by Queen Victoria (with the royal 'our' replacing 'my' in the title). She personifies the takeover of the Highlands by the upper classes for their sporting estates, reducing the native Scots to lackey status. Another is sung by Texas Jim, representing the twentieth-century American proprietorship of much of Scotland's oil resources. He exploits the last line of the original song (as well as the oil) to remind us he is a descendant of a MacAlpine, displaced in the Clearances. There is a savage irony in the fact that, in one sense, it is true that:

> *Yes these are my mountains*
> *And I – have come home.*

But the descendant of a one-time emigrant has intentions that are no different from those of other incomers bent on exploitation.

Another parody, this time of *Bonnie Dundee*, helps satirise the smugly self-righteous Patrick Sellar and James Loch, factor and under-factor to the Sutherland estates. The same melody is also used to subvert Texas Jim and Whitehall in their later exploitation of oil. Government minister Lord Polwarth joins this duo in a subsequent parody of *The Lord of the Dance*. These entertaining re-workings of well-known melodies and lyrics are a key weapon in McGrath's savage satirising of the incoming exploiters, with the audience fully alert to the gap between the worthy sentiments of the original and the self-serving declamations of the parody.

But song is used to quite different effect elsewhere in the play. The haunting Gaelic melodies, coming as they often do after these crude, noisy parodies, are a telling and moving counterpoint to the tawdry self-justifications by the abusers of the land's resources. They connect with the centuries-old traditions of the land and people, underlining the Gaels' enduring dignity in the face of demeaning injustice. Tellingly, it is to them that McGrath leaves the final lines of the play.

The plot is also moved on at times by the singing of existing ballads such as *The Battle of the Braes*, whose re-telling of the fight-back on Skye against Lord Macdonald's evictions dovetails neatly into the play's narrative. Similarly, the song *I will go,* a play-specific version of an older song, carries forward the narrative of the determination of the Land Leaguers to persist in the struggle against the landowners and their broken promises after the First World War.

In harnessing music in various forms to his argument, McGrath demonstrates his acute awareness of its multiple powers: to entertain – obviously – but also to comment, to move, to narrate and, above all, to impose a useful framework on his tale of the land and its people.

 THINGS TO DO AND THINK ABOUT

Interestingly, McGrath leaves the Gaelic songs in the play largely untranslated. One critic has suggested that this is to evoke curiosity. What do you think?

 DON'T FORGET

Be sure you are familiar with the thematic and structural features that McGrath uses to hold the work together. This will help you to tackle the final question when you are asked to identify and analyse links with other parts of the play. A discussion of one or more of these features could form the basis of a good answer.

 VIDEO LINK

Some of the music might not be familiar to you. If this is the case, go to www.brightredbooks.net and watch *I will go* by The Corries for a great version of this song. You can also hear what the music for *The Battle of Harlaw* sounds like. It is the tune for *The Battle of the Braes* in the play.

 ONLINE

A readable analysis of the play can be found on the ASLS website. Key 'McGrath' into the 'Find' box for a useful article by Ali Altun. The link to this can be found at www.brightredbooks.net

 ONLINE TEST

Head to www.brightredbooks.net and take the test on this section.

THE LANGUAGES OF ENGAGEMENT

To support its rapid-fire changes of mood and scene, the play makes use of ever-changing varieties of langu
to present its vision in multiple voices and perspectives. In so doing, it not only adds depth to McGrath's
arguments but also enriches the theatrical experience through constantly-varying modes of expression.

GAELIC

Although present in exchanges between characters at the play's opening, Gaelic gradually disappears from the dialogue, symbolising the fate of the traditional culture of the Highlands within this time frame. Indeed, in the final sketch featuring the twentieth-century crofter and his wife, there is even puzzlement at the use of the word *dram*, underlining the linguistic impoverishment that has been suffered. The constantly recurring use of Gaelic song, however, reminds the audience that the power of its poetry and music to evoke joy and sadness is still alive and undiminished. The call to action in the play's final lines is given to a Gaelic song, deliberately repositioning it as a language of Scotland's potential future.

DRAMATIC IRONY

This is one of McGrath's most potent weapons against the exploiters. The gap between the speaker's words and the audience's knowledge is nowhere more potent than when the third Duke of Sutherland addresses his tenants (p. 46). Unaware of Loch's destructive activities, he speculates how they might feel were the Mongol hordes to *arrive burning your houses, driving you into the sea*. This, of course, is exactly what has been going on in his name. Look also at the judge's summing-up in the case of Patrick Sellar (p. 19). Be alert to McGrath's recurring use of this device whereby the audience's knowledge of events or individuals surpasses that of those speaking.

MUSIC-HALL BANTER

McGrath tells us in his preface to the play that he wishes to avoid the 'lament syndrome', so prevalent in much of Gaelic culture since 1745. He is keen to emphasise the underlying 'energy and vitality' of the people. To capture this energy and vitality, he turns at times to the language and practices of music-hall dialogue and sketch techniques.

For example, the audience joins in with nonsense cries of *Walla, Walla, Wooksie* (p. 25); there are excruciating plays on words/sounds (p. 30) *What shores?/Oh, I'll have a wee dram!* and (p. 26) Frenchman: *Oo are you?/I'm fine, hoo's yersel?*; and wince-making jokes (p. 40) Lady Phosphate: *I quite fancy a small port ... Lord Crask: *Oh – how would you like Lochinver?*

Such dialogue and techniques provide the play with the exuberance McGrath seeks to balance its grimmer moments. It is this interplay of light and dark that keeps the play's forward momentum going and the audience engaged.

EYE-WITNESS ACCOUNTS

Punctuating the humour are numerous eye-witness accounts of brutalities. The flat delivery of reports and statistical information is all the more striking and effective when contrasted with the merriment McGrath conjures up elsewhere. The stark simplicity of the bare facts horrifies (pp. 16–18):

> Donald Sage, Kildonan, Sutherland. The whole inhabitants of Kildonan parish, nearly 2,000 souls, were utterly rooted and burned out. Many, especially the young and robust, left the country, but the aged, the females and children were obliged to stay and accept the wretched allotments allowed them on the seashore and endeavour to learn fishing.

JOURNALISTIC REPORTS

In bringing the story of the exploitation of the land and its people into the twentieth century, McGrath at moments adopts a quasi-BBC reporting technique, as if the audience were watching the *Six O'Clock News*: *In the House of Commons, Willie Hamilton, M.P., said he was not laying charges at the door of any particular individual [...]*

McGrath's selection of facts and figures is presented here in the language of popular journalism, which the audience is familiar with and tends to accept at face value.

POLITICAL INVECTIVE

At moments, particularly towards the end of the play, McGrath adopts the tone of a party political broadcast or meeting, with the actors addressing the audience directly and stridently about what they think must be done:

The people must own the land./The people must control the land. (pp. 65, 72)

We, too, must organise, and fight – not with stones, but politically, with the help of the working classes in the towns, for a government that will control the oil development for the benefit of everybody. (p. 73)

AUDIENCE INVOLVEMENT

Writing in *A Good Night Out* – his manifesto on popular theatre – McGrath voices what he sees as the scope of plays like this one:

'... the theatre can never "cause" a social change. It can articulate pressure towards one, help people celebrate their strengths and maybe build their self-confidence ... Above all, it can be the way people find their voice, their solidarity and their collective determination.'

In this play, we see two ways through which he seeks to help people 'find their voice' and build the 'collective determination' of which he speaks: at times, he invites audience participation through 'collective' singing or joining in with the script; at others, he has his actors step out of character and engage the audience directly.

Both of these techniques are a departure from conventional theatre. McGrath uses them to confront and invite the audience to become involved not only in the performance, but also in the struggle of which (in his eyes) they are a part. For example, the audience is invited through song (p. 1 and p. 9) to join in with expressions of solidarity with the Scottish nation. The Sturdy Highlander in Canada (p. 25) goes even further and has the audience shouting pantomime cries and actions to protect him from danger. Lady Phosphate and Lord Crask later involve the audience – more threateningly this time – by turning their guns directly on them (or is it on us?) in a timely reminder that such people are a danger not only to their tenants but also to others. The play's final moments (pp. 72–74) see the entire company addressing the audience in turn, appealing for their solidarity in the continuing struggle for justice.

Audience involvement plays a significant role in the persuasive structuring of McGrath's case.

ONLINE

The play offers a committed political perspective on the Clearances. To explore other perspectives on these events, follow the link 'The Clearances: Education Scotland' at www.brightredbooks.net. Scroll down to 'The Highland Clearances: Why did So Many People Leave?' and then take the interactive test.

DON'T FORGET

Make sure you can point to the variety of ways in which McGrath avoids what he calls 'the lament syndrome' in telling what is essentially a most troubling narrative.

ONLINE TEST

Want to revise your knowledge of this? Head to www.brightredbooks.net and take the test.

THINGS TO DO AND THINK ABOUT

McGrath is quoted earlier in this section as saying:

'The play is intended, as all our work is, to help people to a greater awareness of their situation and their potential ...'

Organise a class discussion around this statement. Either

1 Examine how Scots might be helped to 'a greater awareness of their situation' by this play. Do you agree that this is the case? Ensure you refer to specific episodes or incidents.

OR

2 What 'greater awareness of their situation' could people from other countries draw from this play? Or is it too Scotland-specific to travel internationally?

Ensure that your points draw on specific episodes or incidents. Look closely before you begin at the section set in Upper Canada (pp. 24–29). Why do you think McGrath has transported some of the action across the Atlantic?

OR

3 Is this play simply socialist propaganda, or is it a successful exercise in theatre craft? Refer to specific episodes or incidents to back up your argument.

If you are not in a position to hold a discussion, list the episodes or incidents which, in your opinion, are most persuasive in helping the audience to this 'greater awareness of their situation'. Comment on how each episode or incident helps you arrive at your opinion.

ENGAGING WITH THE EXTRACT

VIDEO LINK

Watch The Corries singing the original lyrics to *Bonnie Dundee* at www.brightredbooks.net

Now that you have studied the play and explored its themes, its modes of expression and structure, you are ready to look at the type of extract you'll get in the exam. You won't know which particular aspects of the text the extract will highlight, so you need to be prepared for all possibilities. Teacher's comments, study notes and focused discussion in class will all help a great deal, but the best way to prepare is to study the text in your own time, and get to know it really well.

Watch the video, then look at the following extracts and answer the questions that follow.

Here the agents of the Duke of Sutherland contemplate a money-making scheme involving the clearance of a particular area of its population to make way for its repopulation by sheep.

SELLAR: You will really not find this estate pleasant or profitable until by draining to your coast-line or by emigration you have got your mildewed districts cleared. They are just in that state of society for a savage country, such as the woods of Upper Canada – His Lordship should consider seriously the possibility of subsidising their departures. They might even be inclined to carry a swarm of dependants with them.

LOCH: I gather you yourself, Mr Sellar, have a scheme for a sheep-walk in this area.

SELLAR: The highlands of Scotland may sell £200,000 worth of lean cattle this year. The same ground, under the Cheviot, may produce as much as £900,000 worth of fine wool. The effects of such arrangements in advancing this estate in wealth, civilisation, comfort, industry, virtue and happiness are palpable.

Fiddle in – Tune, 'Bonnie Dundee', quietly behind.

LOCH: Your offer for this area, Mr Sellar, falls a little short of what I had hoped.

SELLAR: The present rents, when they can be collected, amount to no more than £142 per annum.

LOCH: Nevertheless, Mr Sellar, His Lordship will have to remove these people at considerable expense.

SELLAR: To restock the land with sheep will cost considerably more.

LOCH: A reasonable rent would be £400 per annum.

SELLAR: There is the danger of disturbances to be taken into account. £300.

LOCH: You can depend on the Reverend David Mackenzie to deal with that. £375.

SELLAR: Mackenzie is a Highlander. £325.

LOCH: He has just been rewarded with the parish of Farr. £365.

SELLAR: I shall have to pay decent wages to my plain, honest, industrious South-country shepherds. £350.

LOCH: You're a hard man, Mr Sellar.

SELLAR: Cash.

LOCH: Done.

They shake hands, then prepare to sing – 'High Industry' *to the tune of* 'Bonnie Dundee'.

LOCH & SELLAR:

As the rain on the hillside comes in from the sea
All the blessings of life fall in showers from me
So if you'd abandon your old misery –
I will teach you the secrets of high industry

Your barbarous customs, though they may be old
To civilised people hold horrors untold –
What value a culture that cannot be sold?
The price of a culture is counted in gold.

contd

Chorus: As the rain, etc.

SELLAR: I've money to double the rent that you pay
The factor is willing to give me my way
So off you go quietly – like sheep as they say –
I'll arrange for the boats to collect you today.

Chorus: As the rain, etc.

LOCH & SELLAR:

Don't think we are greedy for personal gain
What profit we capture we plough back again
We don't want big houses or anything grand
We just want more money to buy up more land.

Chorus: As the rain, etc.

At the end of the song they go off. The GAELIC SINGER stands and says:

SINGER: Mo Dhachaidh (My Home)
She sings the song, in Gaelic. The company and audience join in the chorus.

SINGER: Seinn he-ro-vo, hu-ro-vo hugaibh o he,
So agaibh an obair, bheir togail do m'chridhe,
Bhith stiuireadh mo chasan do m'dhachaidh bheag fhein
Air criochnachadh saothair an là dhomh.

Seall thall air an aiseag am fasgadh nan craobh
Am botham beag geal ud 'se gealaicht le aol
Sud agaibh mo dhachaidh 'se dhachaidh mo ghaoil
Gun chaisteal 's an t-saoghal as fhearr leam.

TRANSLATION:
Seinn he-ro-vo, hu-ro-vo, hugaibh o he,
O this is the work that will raise my heart,
Steering my steps to my own little home,
At the end of my day's labour.

Look yonder beyond the ferry in the shade of the trees,
That little neat lime-whitened cottage,
That's my home; it's the home of my love,
And I prefer it to any castle in the world.

 THINGS TO DO AND THINK ABOUT

Read through the extract above thoroughly before reading and attempting the following questions:

1 Analyse how Sellar's attitude to the local population is made clear in lines 1–5. **3**
2 Throughout their conversation, Loch and Sellar present a series of financial details. By referring to at least two examples, explain how these details are relevant to understanding the concerns of the landowners. **2**
3 By referring closely to the exchange between Loch and Sellar, explain what is revealed about the behaviour of the Church at this time. **2**
4 By referring closely to Loch and Sellar's song, analyse how humour is used in it. **3**
5 Music plays a significant role in the play. By referring to this extract and to others throughout the play, discuss how McGrath has used music and/or song to develop one main theme in the play. **10**

 DON'T FORGET

Note your teacher's comments and your own thoughts in the margins of your own copy of the play. This will really help when you come to revise.

47

GUIDANCE ON POSSIBLE RESPONSES

POSSIBLE RESPONSES TO QUESTION 1

1   Analyse how Sellar's attitude to the local population is made clear in lines 1–5.

Sellar's attitude is one of contempt/disdain for the local population.

Possible evidence to back this up includes any three of:

- *draining to your coastline*: suggests the people who are to be 'drained' away are just like the rubbish/waste you get rid of down a sewer.

- *mildewed districts*: suggests the people are like a destructive/unsightly growth on the areas where they live.

- *in that state of society for a savage country*: suggests they are only fit for living in uncivilised places.

- *a swarm of dependants*: he refers to the people's children as if they were a harmful collection of destructive insects.

POSSIBLE RESPONSES TO QUESTION 2

2   Throughout their conversation, Loch and Sellar present a series of financial details. By referring to at least two examples, explain how these details are relevant to understanding the concerns of the landowners.

Refer to any two of the following:

- £142 is the current rents, but 'when they can be collected' suggests that they are not a reliable source of income.

- £300 suggests that the danger of 'disturbances' cannot be overlooked, meaning the landowners would have to deal with problems caused by unrest/violence from the Highlanders.

- £350 suggests that paying better wages to hard-working southerners would add to their expenses/cost them more.

POSSIBLE RESPONSES TO QUESTION 3

3   By referring closely to the exchange between Loch and Sellar, explain what is revealed about the behaviour of the Church at this time.

- The Church sides with the landowners. (1)

- Its support can be bought/it indulges in financial corruption. (1)

POSSIBLE RESPONSES TO QUESTION 4

4   By referring closely to Loch and Sellar's song, analyse how humour is used in it.

The overriding humour of the song stems from the outrageous irony of this pair imagining that they are a positive force for good in their community when they are in fact destroying it.

Refer to any three of the following:

- *All the blessings of life fall in showers from me*: there is a mad irony in these people seeing themselves as a source of blessings when they are a plague on the life of the Highlands.

- *The secrets of high industry*: again, there is ludicrous irony in seeing the ruining of lives and a culture as being 'high industry' when it is actually destruction.

- *Your barbarous customs*: the irony here stems from the fact that the only barbarous customs we have seen are followed by the landowners, not by the Highlanders.

- *The price of a culture is counted in gold*: this is an outrageous misinterpretation of the value of culture.

- *What profit we capture we plough back again*: this is a topsy-turvy way of viewing land purchase – there is no 'ploughing back' of any kind to add value to the land; the profit goes back into their own holdings. McGrath encourages us to laugh at their outrageous cheek.

POSSIBLE RESPONSES TO QUESTION 5

5   Music plays a significant role in the play. By referring to this extract and to others throughout the play, discuss how McGrath has used music and/or song to develop one main theme in the play.

You can obtain up to 2 marks **either** by finding links to other musical extracts that refer to the **exploitation** of the Highlands **or** to musical interludes referring to the **resistance** by the Highlanders. You would therefore need to refer to other songs that revel in exploitation (for example, those of Lady Phosphate and Lord Crask/Texas Jim/ Lord Polwarth) or to other examples of Gaelic song (or other music) that represent the enduring values and culture of the Highlanders.

You can obtain another 2 marks by referring to the extract given here. You could **either** discuss the crude greed of the exploiters as it emerges here **or** discuss the power of the dignified contrast offered by the traditional Gaelic song that follows, which shows that the exploited view their homeland in a very different way from Loch and Sellar.

You can achieve another 6 marks by discussing similar references (either to the songs of exploitation or to the songs of tradition, depending on the theme you have selected) in at least one other part of the text by McGrath. Think about what these references have in common – for example, theme, characterisation, use of imagery, setting or tone?

 THINGS TO DO AND THINK ABOUT

Remember, there is never any one 'correct' response to these questions. But, when you see 4 marks for a question, think in terms of giving two full responses – each one giving a specific reference followed by a detailed/insightful comment about the text. You'll get no points for just giving a reference. If you think hard, you can always find **something** to say about the reference you have picked out!

JANICE GALLOWAY: *THE TRICK IS TO KEEP BREATHING*

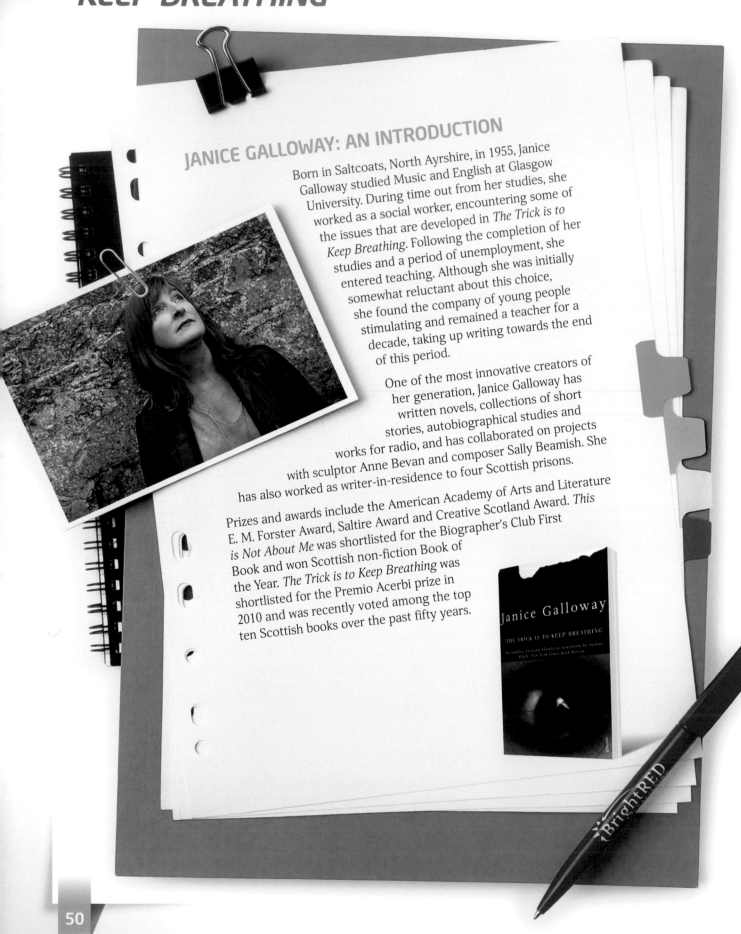

JANICE GALLOWAY: AN INTRODUCTION

Born in Saltcoats, North Ayrshire, in 1955, Janice Galloway studied Music and English at Glasgow University. During time out from her studies, she worked as a social worker, encountering some of the issues that are developed in *The Trick is to Keep Breathing*. Following the completion of her studies and a period of unemployment, she entered teaching. Although she was initially somewhat reluctant about this choice, she found the company of young people stimulating and remained a teacher for a decade, taking up writing towards the end of this period.

One of the most innovative creators of her generation, Janice Galloway has written novels, collections of short stories, autobiographical studies and works for radio, and has collaborated on projects with sculptor Anne Bevan and composer Sally Beamish. She has also worked as writer-in-residence to four Scottish prisons.

Prizes and awards include the American Academy of Arts and Literature E. M. Forster Award, Saltire Award and Creative Scotland Award. *This is Not About Me* was shortlisted for the Biographer's Club First Book and won Scottish non-fiction Book of the Year. *The Trick is to Keep Breathing* was shortlisted for the Premio Acerbi prize in 2010 and was recently voted among the top ten Scottish books over the past fifty years.

OUTLINE

Published in 1989, *The Trick is to Keep Breathing* tells of 27-year-old drama teacher (Joy Stone), and the collapse of identity she suffers after the death of her lover (Michael, a married man) in a swimming accident in Spain while they are on holiday together. The novel traces in great detail the course of her trauma as she desperately tries to make sense of her social, emotional and medical predicament and to find reasons to stay alive after Michael's death. Most damaging to Joy's psyche is what happens at Michael's memorial service, where the officiating minister simply wipes out her existence, extending sympathy only to Michael's estranged wife and ignoring entirely the reality of the life Michael shared with Joy.

This public erasure from her role in Michael's life destroys entirely, in the words of critic Carole Jones, 'her fragile sense of self and effectively contests her entitlement to a place in the world'. As she struggles with the ensuing onset of clinical depression and the anorexia it brings, she finds herself almost entirely on her own, failed by an indifferent health service, handled unsympathetically by an unfeeling housing authority, and prey to the advances of her lecherous boss in her part-time job, to say nothing of the hostile criticisms of an elder sister. This all brings on a crisis in her life, leading to an unprofitable referral to psychiatric ward 1D at Foresthouse Hospital.

Joy doesn't have many people to support her apart from Ellen, the well-meaning but uncomprehending mother of her friend, Marianne, and Marianne herself, who is far away in America. It is David, an ex-pupil at Joy's school, who has the most significant contribution to make as she struggles with her sense of identity. In the end, it is only through her own resilience that Joy finds the will to go on to forge (albeit somewhat tentatively) a new identity for herself.

DON'T FORGET

To get a top grade, you need to know the text intimately, so you'll need to read it several times on your own. It's a good idea to get your own paperback copy, highlight key passages and annotate the margins with comments. This will save you a lot of time when you come to revise.

ONLINE TEST

Head to www.brightredbooks.net and take the test on this section.

VIDEO LINK

Check out the clip 'In Confidence: Janice Galloway' on the Digital Zone.

THINGS TO DO AND THINK ABOUT

Go to www.brightredbooks.net and follow the 'Janice Galloway' link to see her website. Scroll down to 'Resources' and you'll find an early 24-minute TV interview in which she discusses this novel in some detail. She refers to the clip as 'antiquated', but it offers useful insights into this particular text.

JANICE GALLOWAY: NARRATIVE STYLE

DON'T FORGET

All page references are to the Vintage paperback edition of the novel.

Joy's life, as we have seen, has fallen apart. To mirror this disintegration, Galloway's text turns from conventional prose in which one sentence neatly follows another to a narrative style that is as similarly fragmented and fractured as Joy's experience itself. The text is presented in multiple ways and explores a variety of techniques and genres within the framework of a diary-style, first-person narrative. Here are some examples:

- Sometimes sentences are incomplete as the narrator's voice trails into silence, unable to find the words – or will – to continue (for example, pp. 56, 101, 107, 143, 149, 190, 196, 205 and 212).

- Sometimes there are parts of sentences drifting off into the margins of the page as if some stray, recurring thought is hovering on the edge of Joy's consciousness as she talks about something else (for example, pp. 64, 73, 100, 110, 111, 112, 132, 163, 174, 175, 176, 192, 194, 195 and 196). As Joy begins to sharpen her focus on a way forward, these distracting marginal thoughts gradually disappear.

- Sometimes there are almost completely blank pages where a single idea or comment stands out from the surrounding chaos of Joy's feelings (for example, pp. 188 and 202).

- At critical moments, such as the memorial service (pp. 78–79), the page divides into two columns, reflecting the division between the service and Joy's reactions, between Joy and other people.

- Some episodes are presented in playscript form rather than in conventional dialogue, suggesting Joy's divorce and detachment even from herself: she sees herself as a character in a scene rather than as a real, suffering woman (for example, pp. 51–52).

- Joy is an avid reader of women's magazines, and so in the text there are extracts from horoscopes and problem pages (appropriately formatted) that provide an ironic commentary on the gulf between Joy's downbeat reality and upbeat popular journalism. The self-help maxims of magazine titles and self-help manuals recur randomly throughout the text (for example, *You Can't Make Other People Love You Into Existence*; *The More Something Hurts, The More it can Teach Me*). For all their apparent initial triteness, however, they ironically **do** contribute to Joy's eventual stabilisation and renewal: Joy finally finds an identity of her own without it being dependent on someone's love, and it is only the agonising pain of her own experience which shows her a way forward.

- There are nineteen flashbacks (in italics) recounting the events around her lover's death which haunt the text (and Joy) as she relives the agony of those moments.

- There are also other flashbacks of times with her friends Marianne and David and also with Paul, her lover of seven years, which help fill out for the reader a portrait of Joy before Michael's death.

- There are scraps of letters composed to Marianne in America, with Marianne's stridently active life acting as a foil to underline the passive sterility of Joy's existence.

DON'T FORGET

A useful tip for exam preparation might be to look at the titles of articles from magazines and self-help books that Joy quotes, and see which ones actually do come to pay dividends for her.

By experimenting with techniques such as these, Galloway invites the reader into the fragmented mind and troubled life of Joy, to engage with her experience as she lives through it. The very way in which words appear on the page mimics the chaos and confusion of her trauma as she struggles to survive and to keep breathing. At moments of extreme crisis, when her flashbacks reach the moment of the confirmation of Michael's death, the typography is at its most fractured (pages 184–188).

NARRATIVE STRUCTURE

In the interview mentioned earlier in this section, Janice Galloway discusses her approach to novel writing in some detail. Her reluctance to use conventional, continuous prose to describe Joy's progress stems from the fact that much of the novel is taken up with Joy's memories and current feelings. Memories and feelings tend to be, she suggests, 'snapshotic' (her own coined word). In other words, images and moments from the past spring to mind in snapshots, in no sequential order. This, she feels, is a surer way to bring Joy alive for us: using continuous prose with its structured, formal sentences and paragraphs would, she believes, convey a false idea of organisation in a mind struggling with emotional and psychological breakdown.

This, of course, confronts the novelist with a problem: while this approach effectively simulates Joy's psychological disintegration, the reader does need some kind of structure to follow events. Galloway solves this problem through skilful use of encounters and flashbacks.

ENCOUNTERS

Galloway shapes her narrative by introducing encounters with various members of society. Each encounter in its different way underlines Joy's isolation and alienation, deprived as she is from almost any kind of understanding or support. The encounters pinpoint the multiple problems Joy has to face at a professional, social, medical and emotional level at this traumatic moment in her life.

FLASHBACKS

We need to know a lot more about Joy and her life before this painful episode if we are to be able to understand and engage with her. For example, how did she become the person who is Joy Stone? How did she live her life before Michael's death? What was her personality like in earlier times? To answer these questions, Janice Galloway intersperses Joy's numerous encounters with flashbacks – not simply to Michael's death – but to a pre-Michael period when a biographical context gradually emerges to present a fuller picture of the novel's central character.

ONLINE

Read more about Janice Galloway by following the British Council link at www.brightredbooks.net

ONLINE TEST

How well have you learned this topic? Take the test at www.brightredbooks.net

THINGS TO DO AND THINK ABOUT

Once you have completed your first reading, make a list of the various encounters Joy has in the course of the novel. Consider how each one contributes to Joy's mental and/or emotional state at any given moment.

JOY'S WORLD 1

As the novel unfolds, Galloway skilfully draws us into Joy's world. It is a world which we might initially be reluctant to enter, given its miseries and anxieties. But we are gradually won over by the many facets Galloway gives to Joy and her life. We are continually discovering new dimensions to her. By making us familiar with aspects of Joy's background and experience, and by enriching her character portrayal with insights into her innermost thoughts and fears, Galloway ensures that we are ultimately caught up in the fate of this complex woman.

FAMILY BACKGROUND

No real mention of family comes until nearly sixty pages into the narrative, suggesting in itself that family is irrelevant to Joy at this troubled time. The first family encounter (p. 57) is far from being a source of comfort. The sudden appearance of Myra, her much older sister, fills Joy with wild panic and despair, and their history of failed communication and lurking hostility is revealed (pp. 58–72).

Relations with her mother were apparently similarly unsupportive. While Joy had paid for a telephone (p. 56) for her ageing mother, it had apparently done little to assist mutual communication; later (p. 189) we learn of harsh recriminations by the mother against a teenage Joy. Myra claims (p. 67) that Joy 'never gret for [her] mother', when she died, calling her 'a callous bitch'. (Myra, however, is drunk at this point, and her reliability as a witness is therefore open to question.) Joy's father died of drink when she was five.

Apparently, there are no fewer than five female members who have committed suicide (p. 199). This suggests a family that is serially challenged by depressive tendencies, and helps us to understand that Joy's depression, while triggered by Michael's death, forms part of a recurring family pattern. Family, it appears in this novel, is not seen as a potential source of support. The negative information we gather about Joy's family only adds to the comic irony in Chapter 3 where the self-help book Joy is reading (p. 171) encourages her to 'get my family around me. They will be a great source of strength and comfort if I let them.'

RELATIONS WITH MEN

Although Michael's death is the cause of Joy's emotional devastation, he is not the only man with whom she has been, and is, associated.

PAUL

Pages 41–44 detail a seven-year relationship with Paul (whom she met at school) and from whom she became increasingly estranged as they each matured in their different ways. At this point in her life, Joy sees cooking and cleaning for her man as a means of promoting her desirability. She defines herself as a woman in terms of her usefulness to Paul. When Paul moves on, she feels her identity is thrown into question. When he finally proves to her that she no longer serves any useful purpose in his life, she tells us: 'I don't think I ever came to terms with the shock' (p. 43). This is the first step on the slide to her identity crisis.

contd

MICHAEL

Michael, a teacher at Joy's school, leaves his wife after she discovers his affair with Joy. Hurt by the failure of her dependency-driven relationship with Paul, she seems keen for this new relationship to be different, telling us how important it is for each partner to have his/her own independent home: 'When he came to me or I to him, it would be from choice' (p. 65). Despite her desire for non-dependency, Joy's utter collapse after Michael's death suggests that she was still wholly dependent on the man in her life to define herself as a woman. (This feeling of non-existence is compounded when she is further stripped of identity by being glossed over completely at Michael's memorial service.) Without him, she disintegrates entirely in a way that goes far beyond grief at the death of a loved one. She has not just suffered the loss of a partner, but the loss of her identity, too.

TONY

Tony is Joy's boss at her part-time job in a bookmaker's. The married Tony is the stereotypical male chauvinist, seeing Joy simply as a convenient sex object. 'Tony strokes my hair when he is in a good mood and tells them [the customers in the bookie's shop] I'm a pet' (p. 32). Tony's sexist treatment of Joy is patently demeaning to her as a woman, but for much of the novel she passively accepts the role which Tony has allotted her. Finding herself the object of his crass attentions, she tells us: 'I'm supposed to smile and I do.'

When Tony asks her out, Joy's beautifying preparations take several pages (pp. 46–48). By way of explanation for this lengthy ritual, she tells us: 'Maybe I will be embraced, entered, *made to exist*' (p. 46). This latter phrase suggests that, as with Paul and Michael, in her own eyes at least, her existence as a woman depends on her relationship with a man. It is a key moment in her gradual discovery of her own selfhood when we hear her saying 'no' to Tony's attentions (p. 209). She has taken a hesitant, but vital, first step towards accepting herself as a woman in her own right, defined in her own terms, not in those of any man she may encounter.

DAVID

David is a college student, an ex-pupil at Cairdwell Secondary (Joy's school). It is significant that he is ten years Joy's junior, and comes from a different generation to the other men in Joy's life. He brings a new kind of masculinity to the novel – one that gives rather than takes. He is concerned for Joy after her mother's funeral, accompanies her to Michael's memorial service and visits her in hospital. It is David who first articulates (to Ellen) the advice that Joy will only understand much later: 'She shouldn't get dependent on any one person again. Not on one person' (p. 132). For the moment, however, Joy is uncomprehending. 'I didn't know what he meant' (p. 132).

It is David's unannounced visit on her birthday that halts a suicide attempt. While Tony's sexual interest in Joy is self-serving, David's is supportive, helping her get through the grief and pain of Michael's death. 'We get drunk and have sex and I scream a lot of the time [...] He takes the screaming and holds me' (p. 133). Towards the novel's end, as we observe Joy's social life gradually broadening through increasing contact with colleagues from school, David helps Joy towards that state of non-dependency on any one person by quietly effacing himself into the background.

 ## THINGS TO DO AND THINK ABOUT

A useful way to revise and deepen your knowledge of the text might be to organise a group discussion (or write an essay) under the heading 'What does Janice Galloway have to say in this novel about relationships between men and women?' Make sure you have plenty of textual evidence to back up your main points.

 DON'T FORGET

Be ready in the exam to compare or contrast the behaviour of one man with another in their treatment of Joy. Also, be prepared to discuss the behaviour of any one man towards Joy. Is his treatment consistent throughout the novel, or does it change in any way?

 ONLINE

Head to www.brightredbooks.net to read an interesting article Janice Galloway wrote about another novel of hers – *Clara*. Do you see any links between Joy and Galloway's descriptions of Clara?

ONLINE TEST

Want to revise your knowledge of this? Head to www.brightredbooks.net and take the test.

JOY'S WORLD 2

IDENTITY, GUILT AND UNFULFILLED EXPECTATIONS

For Joy, fulfilling the expectations of others extends beyond emotional relationships with men. A constant theme in the novel is Joy's desire to please everyone she meets. Throughout the novel, she conceals her own desires and attempts to live up to what she feels is expected of her: for Ellen, she pretends to eat and enjoy the food prepared for her (despite her anorexia); for the health visitor, she makes elaborate tea arrangements, pretending to her that she is managing; for her sister, she also pretends to be coping, although this is far from the reality; for Marianne, her friend absent in America, she makes similarly reassuring remarks such as 'Nobody needs to worry about me' (p. 109). Her life is a constant round of living up to what she feels is expected of her in her bereaved position. Her frequent failures in her own eyes lead to a sense of guilt. By attempting to live up to the expectations of others, Joy is desperately trying to create an identity to live in, to make up for the one that she has lost – that of being Michael's partner. This loss is further cruelly emphasised at his memorial service (p. 79). The novel details her long, difficult progress to a rediscovered sense of self, free from guilt and the expectations of others.

DON'T FORGET

Joy has a complex character. Make notes about her character traits, and find references and quotations that exemplify these. You will need to be able to point to a reference or quotation which exemplifies the character trait under discussion.

THE DIVIDED SELF

It is no coincidence that Joy divides her time between two homes: her own cottage and Michael's council house. The cottage represents her own identity; Michael's home represents the displacement of her own identity. It is a measure of her rediscovery of her own identity that the novel's final pages see her going back to her own cottage, facing up to the problem of dry rot (partly symbolic of the condition that had overtaken her) and planning how best to rectify recent neglect.

But the division extends to more than that between two homes, for, in the very first line of the novel, we see a split in Joy herself. We find her watching herself as if she were someone else, so intense is her loss of identity. 'I watch myself from the corner of the room' (p. 7). When she looks in the bathroom mirror, she says it is 'like looking through a window at someone else' (p. 10). She likes her work, since she can be similarly divorced from herself. 'I can be outside myself, watching from the corner of the room' (p. 12). And, before going out with Tony, she inspects herself in the mirror and smiles 'at the woman in the mirror. Her eyes are huge. But what looks back is never what I want' (p. 48). She has lost a sense of her real self, and what she sees in its place is alien and unappealing. (Remember, too, Joy's tendency to cast herself as a person in a play, further suggesting the divide between her actual reality and an imagined projection of herself.)

Joy finally conquers her demons by learning from her prolonged suffering that 'The trick is not to think. Just act dammit' (p. 207). It is after this realisation that she returns, not only to her cottage, but to a sense of inner wholeness, too.

JOY'S HUMOUR

No discussion of the novel would be complete without commenting on Galloway's humour. Admittedly, it is humour of a black nature; but it forms an integral part of Joy's vision of the world, rounding out her character for the reader. What might have been an emotional landscape too bleak for many readers to take is rescued by Joy's gleeful sense of the ridiculous and her self-mocking commentary. Relishing the ironic gap between the relentlessly positive comments in magazines and self-help books and her own situation is just one facet of this. Wishing extravagantly one moment for non-existence, she cries:

'Please god make boulders crash through the roof. In three or four days when the Health Visitor comes she will find only mashed remains, marrowbone jelly oozing between the shards like bitumen. *Well,* she'll say, *We're not doing so well today, are we?'* (p. 84)

We warm to a character who can still find ironic, black humour in her nightmarish situation. This is not only necessary for the reader; it is also necessary for Joy's sanity when she is faced with the ghastly realities of her long journey to personal renewal.

 THINGS TO DO AND THINK ABOUT

To consolidate your knowledge of Joy's life circumstances, arrange a group discussion based around the question: 'By what means does Janice Galloway win our sympathy for Joy?' Consider not only her various relationships but also her living arrangements and professional life. Base your comments on textual evidence, and avoid generalisations. Note the points that arise during the discussion.

 ONLINE TEST

Head to www.brightredbooks.net and take the test on this section.

 ONLINE

Check out the resources at www.brightredbooks.net for more on *The Trick is to Keep Breathing.*

ENGAGING WITH THE EXTRACT

You have now had time to study the story itself, the narrative style and structure, the key characters, the themes and the character of Joy herself. The extract in the exam will draw on some of these features of your study. As we've said before, you won't know which aspects of the text you'll be examined on. Your teacher's comments, study notes and focused discussion in class will all help a great deal, but the best way to prepare is to study the text in your own time, and get to know it really well.

Read the following extract and then answer the questions that follow.

In the novel's final pages, Joy takes stock of her present situation as she contemplates her future.

1 The whisky. The tree lights. Wee diversions. I find a glass before I let myself sit then open the presents in the correct order. First things first. The box for the lights sifts tinsel stuff down the front of my jeans and onto the carpet. Very festive. I have to take the plug off the turntable to try them out though. Sip of whisky then stand back. They work first time. Pretty
5 pinks and greens, yellow and blue, glitter on the shades making sparks. I turn to the window and see the house interior ghosted on the black outside: the yellow walls boiling with colour.

No radio.

Takes a minute to remember I left it at the cottage, near the hallway door. It'll be dark over there. All that peeled-back paper hanging from the bedroom walls. I can always clean the
10 worst of the visible damage, strip and wash the walls, open the doors to let winter air refresh. I can leave all the windows open as well: there's nothing anyone would come in and steal. I can paint the window frames white again, lift the carpet tile in the hall with a scarf over my nose and mouth. I'll make lists. Things that need to be done for the next week or so. The week after that.

15 After that.

Tomorrow.

David will come. I may visit Ellen.

But tonight I have no radio.

I find the Walkman and riffle tapes. Wee bit of Debussy. I lock it into place, fit the
20 headphones. The battery light bleeds. A clicking in the ears as breath escapes in a white curl. Cold enough to snow. I could get the duvet maybe. Later. Tree lights throw colours on the wall and whisky washes wide in my chest as
the music comes through.

The lights and this sound.

25 Maybe

Maybe I could learn to swim.

Another mouthful, picturing the sea. Casting out long arms into the still water. I am naked, hair long as a fin down the pale spine ridge, flexible as a fish, the white profile against the black waves, rising for air.

30 A little light fiction.

Shadows in the corner of the room give me away. I'm gawky, not a natural swimmer. But I can read up a little, take advice. I read somewhere the trick is to keep breathing, make out it's not unnatural at all. They say it comes with practice.

I take another mouthful of whisky, slide my finger on the volume control. Waves rippling
35 through the headphones.

And something else.

The human voice. I listen watching the coloured lights, fanning like sea anemones over the ceiling, till the music stops.

A click and tape whirring into silence at the end of the reel.

40   The voice is still there.
    I forgive you.

I hear it quite distinctly, my own voice in the empty house.
    I forgive you.

Nobody needs to know I said it. Nobody needs to know.

45   The tape winds on into empty space. Inside the headphones I hear the rise and fall, the surf beating in my lungs. Reach for the bottle. Watch the lights.

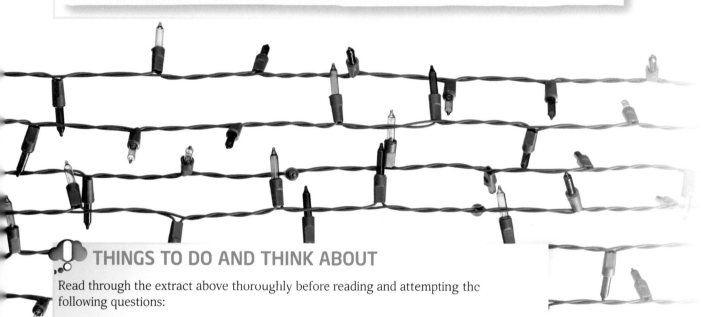

THINGS TO DO AND THINK ABOUT

Read through the extract above thoroughly before reading and attempting the following questions:

1 By referring closely to the first two paragraphs, analyse how Janice Galloway conveys Joy's current mood.   **4**

2 By referring to at least two examples, analyse how the author employs sentence structure in lines 14–26 to suggest how Joy views the future.   **4**

3 Explain why lines 40–44 mark a significant moment in Joy's view of herself.   **2**

4 With reference to setting and characterisation, discuss how this extract contrasts with the presentation of Joy elsewhere in the novel.   **10**

 **DON'T FORGET**

Detail is what will bring you marks in this type of question. Structure your answers around specific words and phrases.

GUIDANCE ON POSSIBLE RESPONSES

POSSIBLE RESPONSES TO QUESTION 1

1 By referring closely to the first two paragraphs, analyse how Janice Galloway conveys Joy's current mood.

You should first recognise that Joy is in quite a positive/creative/ practical/forward-looking mood, taking an interest in her surroundings and future plans in a way she did not do before.

Possible answers include:

- *The whisky/Sip of whisky then stand back*: Alcohol is seen as part of a celebration/ reward rather than an escape mechanism as before. Part of her *wee diversions*.
- *The tree lights*: She goes to some trouble to get lights to work. At the start of the novel she preferred to sit in the dark, avoiding any kind of light. Here she's trying to create a more cheerful atmosphere.
- *tinsel stuff down the front of my jeans [...] Very festive*: She enjoys the sparkle of the mess.
- *Pretty pinks and greens, yellow and blue, glitter on the shades*: These bright colours contrast sharply with the previous general drabness of her domestic surroundings, suggesting a brightening of mood as well of surroundings.
- *the yellow walls boiling with colour*: Here imagery of heat and colour are present, both somewhat lacking before, suggesting a more upbeat mood.
- *I can* + verb: repetition of parallel structures with regard to her future plans (*clean, strip and wash, open, paint, lift*). All references here are to fixing up/getting her surroundings into order. Until now, she has neglected them. This hints at a more positive view of her future.
- *I'll make lists*: These lists of future activities are different from Joy's previous lists. Before, lists were simply to fill the grim gaps in her time; here they sound more like real plans for future action.

POSSIBLE RESPONSES TO QUESTION 2

2 By referring to at least two examples, analyse how the author employs sentence structure in lines 15–26 to suggest how Joy views the future.

Possible answers include:

- *The week after that*: Minor sentence that halts without deciding on a definite plan, suggesting in its vagueness the expanding possibilities of future action, something lacking in Joy's life for much of the novel.
- *After that*: Again, the brief minor sentence in its lack of precise outcome captures now – not the emptiness of Joy's life as before, but the limitless possibilities ahead of her.
- *Tomorrow*: The single-word sentence is left hanging in the air to emphasise its importance. The single-word sentence underlines the fact that 'Tomorrow' is a concept she can now contemplate and relish. Before, she lived partly in the past, partly in the present. The future ('Tomorrow') didn't really then exist for her. Now it does.
- *David will come*: The brevity of the sentence here catches an assured certainty about her future, absent for much of her previous life.
- *I may visit Ellen*: The use of 'may' in this brief sentence underlines the relaxed confidence with which she contemplates her future choices.
- *Tree lights throw colours on the wall and whisky washes wide in my chest as*

  the music comes through: 'the music comes through' is placed in a separate line in the original text to emphasise the music's importance in Joy's relish of the moment. Debussy's music also helps her to approach an extremely difficult idea for her: the contemplation of water not as a destructive element but as a liberating one. (She also refers later on to being 'flexible as a fish'.)

- *The lights and this sound*: By appearing in a minor sentence of their own, the lights and music are highlighted to show their growing importance in Joy's thoughts at the moment. 'lights' is the final word in the novel, suggesting Joy's progress from the spiritual dark into a brighter future; the 'sound' is the sound of the sea in Debussy's *La Mer*, suggesting that water, the element that took Michael from her, is something she no longer contemplates with horror, but with a lightness of touch.
- *Maybe*

  Maybe I could learn to swim: This layout on the page emphasises with its repeat of the 'maybe'

  (but with a great pause between the two) the tentative nature of the enormity of what Joy is proposing to herself – learning to swim, an activity which took Michael from her. She later calls this 'a little light fiction'; but the fact that she could – even facetiously – contemplate such an idea shows how far she has come.

POSSIBLE RESPONSES TO QUESTION 3

3 Explain why lines 40–44 mark a significant moment in Joy's view of herself.

For much of the novel, Joy has tried to live up to the expectations many people had of her: her mother, the health visitor, her headteacher, the doctors and Tony (to name only a few). She failed, and felt guilt at failing to live up what was expected of her. The fact that she hears her own voice (twice) saying *I forgive you* marks a turning point in her self-image, allowing a progression to a more positive view of herself and of her future.

POSSIBLE RESPONSES TO QUESTION 4

4 With reference to setting and characterisation, discuss how this extract contrasts with the presentation of Joy elsewhere in the novel.

You can obtain up to 2 marks by identifying elements of commonality in past setting and characterisation that contrast with the present ones.

You can achieve a further 2 marks for referring to the extract here.

You will be awarded 6 additional marks for discussing contrasting references to at least one other part of the text by the author.

Here are some possible contrasting references:

- In the opening paragraphs of the novel, Joy sits in the dark and cold, actively avoiding light in a depressingly unpleasant room (setting). Joy's mood is similarly dark; she is fearful and without any comfort. There is no talk of people or of the future.
- Here there is a contrasting reference to the light and colour of her Christmas lights. There is enjoyment here, of music and whisky. There is also talk of future plans for her home, involvement with friends and future activity.
- In the opening scene, we are told *Brightness disagrees with me*, so she sits in the dark, the only light coming from moonlight and streetlights behind the closed curtains. The room is comfortless: the carpet is wet and *seeps*, and the draught from the attic filters through and *makes me cold*. This chilly setting also contributes to the characterisation of Joy herself, being without pleasure or comfort, with no mention of future prospects except that *something terrible might happen*.
- In this extract, we find Joy enjoying the coloured Christmas lights, savouring the *pretty pinks and greens*, with Joy's domestic interior lights now brightening a *black outside*. She also has a *sip of whisky* as she contemplates in a relaxed way the repairs she will make to her home to get it back into a comfortable order. She is also contemplating various social possibilities (*David will come. I may visit Ellen*), She even contemplates learning to swim – not too seriously (*A little light fiction*), but there is no doubting her positive view of the future which contrasts starkly with the horrors of her then present at the novel's start.

THINGS TO DO AND THINK ABOUT

When you see 4 marks for a question, think in terms of giving two full responses – each one giving a specific reference followed by a detailed/insightful comment about the text.

DON PATERSON

PATERSON: AN INTRODUCTION

Born in Dundee in 1963, Don Paterson was, in his early years, more drawn to music than to the written word. He left school at 16 and, like his father before him, worked for a local newspaper publisher before his musical skills drew him in 1984 to London, where he played and recorded with the award-winning folk-jazz group, Lammas. It was at the age of 20 that he began to take a serious interest in poetry after discovering the poet Tony Harrison.

Paterson gave over a year of his life to reading poetry and steeping himself in the tradition of British poets before he began to write and publish his own work. Success came with his first collection of poems, *Nil Nil* (1993), which won the Forward Prize for Best First Collection. Other prestigious awards followed: *God's Gift to Women* (1997) won both the T. S. Eliot Prize and the Geoffrey Faber Memorial Prize, and *Landing Light* (2003) won the Whitbread Poetry Award and, most unusually, a second T. S. Eliot Prize. He has also won the Arvon Foundation International Poetry Competition, an Eric Gregory Award, three Book Awards from the Scottish Arts Council, and a Creative Scotland Award.

In 2008, he was appointed Officer of the Order of the British Empire for his services to literature. He is a fellow of the Royal Society of Literature; and his collection *Rain* won the Queen's Poetry Medal in 2009.

He works for the publisher Picador as poetry editor, and also teaches creative writing at the University of St Andrews.

DON PATERSON
Nil Nil

PATERSON: THE POET

Writing in *How Poets Work*, Paterson comments: '... the poet's job is to make the commonplace miraculous'. And this is, indeed, what he does. The poems that we encounter here for Higher English present us with commonplace items such as football matches, pool tables, bus journeys, fruit trees and even a half-pint of Guinness and a gallstone. But, for Paterson, 'the commonplace' is only an entry point, believing as he does that 'what you're talking about has got to be transformed at the end of the poem', adding that the poem is a kind of 'pilgrimage, some transforming process that the reader has to make with you'. In other words, 'the commonplace' he talks of earlier has to help the reader to view the familiar with new eyes. And, to take the reader on this 'pilgrimage', Paterson sometimes uses traditional forms such as the sonnet, while at others he crafts his own forms, paying great attention to technical elements such as rhyme and metre, reflecting the discipline of his musical grounding.

As one of the best-read poets working in Britain today, Paterson is well-equipped to make allusions to other literatures, cultures and sub-cultures. Often, he delights in confronting the reader with bizarre, playful connections between the exotically unusual and the everyday which are, as critic Roderick Watson comments, 'typical of Paterson's capacity to amuse, challenge, disturb and be lyrical in equal measure'. But, for Paterson, a poem should do even more; he sees it as having a 'real power to actually inspire readers to think or live differently'. We're now going to examine the extent to which he achieves this aim.

 THINGS TO DO AND THINK ABOUT

When you read these poems in class, you will be reading them from several of Paterson's collections of poetry. If you type them out now, you'll have your own copy of each poem in one complete set that you can use to highlight and mark up metaphors, similes, enjambment, rhyme schemes, key quotations, words and phrases. You can also add notes and comments.

Creating your own set of poems will also help you to spot links between the extract you are given and one or more other poems in the selection, a skill vital for success in the high-value final Scottish Texts question. You'll be able to check up quickly on parallels or contrasts in subject matter, form, themes/ideas or poetic devices.

Getting your poetry file organised **now** could save you a lot of time searching for revision material at exam time. And that could make a big difference to your final grade.

 ONLINE

One way to enrich your study of Don Paterson's poetry is to listen to his music-making. Visit the link at www.brightredbooks.net and click on the music tab at the top right-hand side of the page. The tracks are as highly individual and evocative as his poetry.

 DON'T FORGET

'Lyrical' – the adjective used by critic Roderick Watson – is a useful one for discussing or writing about poems such as Don Paterson's *Waking with Russell* and *The Thread*. It describes poetry in which the poet expresses his most personal emotions. Lyrical poetry often employs the sort of specific rhyming schemes that we find in the sonnet, for example. It's a useful word for Critical Reading and critical essays.

 ONLINE TEST

Head to www.brightredbooks.net and take the test on this section.

WAKING WITH RUSSELL AND THE THREAD

WAKING WITH RUSSELL

SUBJECT

This poem is about the joy and sense of renewal the poet feels on waking up in bed to the smile of his four- day-old son, Russell, whose twin brother is the subject of *The Thread*.

FORM: SONNET

Here we see Paterson's mastery of form at work. Although the inspiration for the form is the 14-line Italian sonnet, with its eight-line *octave* followed by its six-line *sestet*, Paterson adapts the form, quite radically, to his own purposes here.

The major difference to note in the rhyme scheme is that he abandons the traditional Italian sonnet rhyme scheme (*abba, abba, cd, cd, cd* or *cde, cde*) for one dependent on half-rhyme.

Half-rhyme is formed by words with similar but not identical sounds. In *Waking with Russell*, Paterson gives us half-rhymes on *began, again, grin, cammin, ran, on, men.* The ending consonant sound (or *consonance*) is the same ('n') but the vowel sounds are different, yet related in each word.

We see something similar on the alternating lines with *lovers, waver, rediscovered, ever, giver, river, forever.*

This very personal rhyme scheme (an *abab* format throughout) binds the sonnet together even more tightly than usual, which is appropriate for a poem celebrating the physical and emotional closeness of father and son. Paterson's subtlety with unifying half-rhymes merges form and subject matter powerfully yet unobtrusively.

Traditionally, the octave and sestet set out two contrasting attitudes or states of mind; and here Paterson follows convention: for example, 'the difference' mentioned in the first line is made clear in the last two lines of the octave and in the first line of the sestet.

Compare the difference between

Dear son, I was mezzo del cammin
and the true path was as lost to me as ever

and

when you cut in front and lit it as you ran.

Here the turn from octave to sestet sees Paterson moving on from mid-life loss of direction to a clear path ahead illuminated by his joy in his son's smile.

Typically, the rhythm of a sonnet line uses iambic pentameters – that is, five 'bars', each with a weak syllable followed by a strong one:

I kissed / your mouth / and pledged / myself / forever.

Although Paterson uses iambic pentameter to shape the overall rhythmic pattern, he does not follow it slavishly. Rather, he departs from it as necessary to maintain the conversational tone that he prizes in this most personal of poetic forms. In his essay *The Dilemma of the Poet* (1997), he wrote: 'I don't want the reader ever to be aware of the metre or the rhyme scheme.' We will see this is a hallmark of his style in this and other poems.

COMMENT

Here, Paterson explores the sonnet's love poem roots (*face-to-face like lovers*). But, playfully, he subverts our expectations: the 'lovers' are a father and his four-day old son whom we find together *waking amongst men.* (And for the father the *waking* has a metaphorical sense, as he opens his eyes to seeing *the true path* more clearly now). Paterson makes here one of his startling trade-mark connections: between everyday Kirriemuir and the more exotic world of the *Divine Comedy* of Dante (1265-1321) whose first lines translated read:

Midway on our life's journey, (mezzo del cammin) *I found myself*

In dark woods, the right road lost.

Cleverly, Paterson uses, and then adds to, the 'road' imagery of Dante when his son 'cut in', like a car driver in a hurry, another example of Paterson's fondness for making unlikely connections, here between 13th century Italy and our contemporary world.

An aphorism is a concise observation that contains a general truth. Paterson here couches one of the poem's key ideas in one; Russell's smile which *dawned on him,* also brought light to the father: *See how the true gift never leaves the giver.* To underline the strength of this *true gift* at the heart of the poem, Paterson employs rugged alliteration. The gift was *returned and redelivered, it rolled on* until the smile's strength was such that it *poured through us like a river,* the repeated 'r' sound catching a new energetic forward drive, contrasting sharply with the father's stalled movement earlier. And contrasting equally sharply with

contd

this energy is the quiet tenderness in the last line where the iambic pentameter beat, which has unobtrusively governed the poem's rhythm, falls with gentle finality on the on key words in the final line (see 'Form' section).

ONLINE

Jamie is Russell's twin. Paterson writes powerfully about the difficulties of Jamie's birth on his website. He also writes humorously about being the father of twins. To find out more, key in www.donpaterson.com in your browser, then click on the 'Other writing' tab at the top of the website, scroll down to 'Poetry' and click on 'Landing Light – PBS Bulletin'.

THE THREAD

SUBJECT

Paterson expresses gratitude and wonder at the now-robust health of Russell's twin, Jamie, whose life – at the time of his birth – had been held only by a thread.

FORM: SONNET

Again, we see Paterson using the 14-line Italian sonnet (complete with octave and sestet) as the basis for his own version. Here, he employs the rhyme scheme of *abba, cdde, fgh, hgf* and he dips in and out of full, and half-rhyme as it suits his purpose.

The first four lines (or quatrain) of the octave look back to the frightening circumstances of Jamie's birth, with the uncertainties of the birth mirrored in the halting rhythm of the first three lines, and the surer rhythm of the iambic pentameter only appearing in line 4 when Jamie's life is out of danger.

The next four lines describe Paterson's thankfulness that he, Russell and Jamie (now restored to full health) can enjoy their energetic game of 'aeroplanes' as they roar down Kirrie Hill. The happiness and heartiness of this moment of togetherness between a father and his two sons is underlined by Paterson's use of full rhyme throughout this quatrain (*will, hill / Russ, us*).

The end of the sestet sees Paterson reflecting on the contrast between the past and the present: the thread of life which only just held Jamie at birth is now sufficiently strong to bind the whole family together. Because of the reflective nature of much of the poem, Paterson employs the rhythm of the iambic pentameter very flexibly (at times it is present and at times it's not) to follow the fluctuations in his train of thought.

COMMENT

The poem is held together by a framework of two extended metaphors, one based on flying, the other on the poem's title, *The Thread*. That aeroplane engines and a fragile thread should come together in a single poem highlight Paterson's delight in making unlikely, but memorable, connections.

Like a plane landing badly, Jamie *ploughed straight back into the earth* at the moment of his birth, (with *earth* carrying connotations of both grave and growth). Growth prevailed, as did *the thread of his one breath* and here he is now, part of *the great twin-engined swaying wingspan of us* (*us*: Russell, Jamie and father), with an energy in his lungs *out-revving / every engine in the universe* as they race downhill. The incongruity between a roaring twin-engined 'plane' and *the thread of his one breath* underlines the contrast between a present robustness an earlier fragility. The once delicate thread is now strong enough that it is now *holding all of us*: father, *the white dot of your mother,* and the two boys, a unifying force of great strength.

THINGS TO DO AND THINK ABOUT

To revise, list the points you might make in a group discussion on the contrasts and similarities of these two poems. Consider subject matter, use of form and the mood of the speaker in each case. Note any changes in mood in individual poems. How does Paterson create these changes?

ONLINE TEST

How well have you learned this topic? Take the test at www.brightredbooks.net

11.00 *BALDOVAN* AND *TWO TREES*

11.00 BALDOVAN

SUBJECT

This is from a collection of poems in which Paterson picks some titles from various stops on the defunct Dundee-to-Newtyle railway. This poem, however, is about a short bus trip made by two small boys. The two stops mentioned – Macalpine Road and Hilltown – are about 20 minutes apart in his native Dundee. Nevertheless, for the 'I' of the poem, this seems like an extraordinary adventure, comparable to leaving base camp to climb a mountain, a journey fraught with terrors in his young mind.

FORM: COUPLET

In this poem, Paterson employs the couplet, a traditional poetic form. He seems to be enjoying a quiet joke by using a form often associated with epic poems about heroes such as Odysseus or Beowulf to describe a bus trip by two small boys. As with the sonnet form, he adapts the couplet form to suit his own purpose.

Traditionally, couplets are made up of two lines that rhyme and have the same number of 'beats'. In other words, they are firmly controlled in rhyme and rhythm. However, Paterson is writing in the voice of a small boy for whom this regularity would be totally unnatural. So he adapts it, and uses half-rhymes such as *boys/ terminus, Hilltown/ own, forget/ sites, Road/ dead* to capture, conversationally, the speaker's thoughts and fears, only allowing a few full rhymes to appear from time to time. He leaves lines with variable lengths and stresses, adding still more to the colloquial tone. The couplet format, however, keeps a loose controlling hand on the overall structure.

COMMENT

If we work from the assumption that the 'I' of the poem is Don Paterson himself (born in 1963) and that many of the coins mentioned were no longer legal tender after decimalisation in 1971, then we can put the speaker's age at around 8. Yet, there is a dual perspective. We hear the voice of the eight-year-old: *I plan to buy comics/ sweeties, and magic tricks*, but immediately after the small boy's word choice there follows the more sophisticated vocabulary of the adult, affectionately remembering his younger self and his concerns: *However, I am obscurely worried as usual/ over matters of procedure, the protocol of travel.*

Throughout the poem, there is this curious mix of schoolboy expression (*me and Ross Mudie*) with more exotic phrases (*the cold blazonry of the half-crown*; 'blazonry': coat of arms; 'half-crown': 25 pence).

But the character of the schoolboy (and his neuroses) is well established as he sets out: he has been *weighing up* a large collection of various coins to fund this expedition from *Base Camp* which *chank* (in glorious onomatopoeia) *like thick cogs.* Yet he still worries if he has enough. His anxieties emerge in a series of questions to Ross, which begin with everyday concerns (*where we should sit*) and build to a climax as they approach Hilltown: *Are ye sure? Are you sure?* The adult voice takes over briefly at this point: *I cannot know the little good it do me;/ the bus will let us down in another country.*

From here, the boy's worries fly off in a whirlwind of fears. His panic can be heard in the enjambment which takes over; the next twelve lines are all one sentence, as his nightmare vision of what awaits them mounts hysterically. He first imagines them hopelessly lost, then frighteningly misunderstood in this strange, other country, before returning to some post-nuclear-holocaust version of their former homes.

The speaker's terrors are both reasonable and understandable if you remember that boys of this age are often familiar with science-fiction comics, and that in this pre-1971

contd

world, the Cold War was at its height and nuclear annihilation was a commonly discussed possibility. While we may smile at his child-like idea of acid rain tasting of *kelly* (sherbet), the apocalyptic vision he conjures up from a commonplace starting point is nevertheless chillingly convincing of the dreads of the imaginative child. While the poem amuses in places, it also disturbs, in the way which Professor Watson suggested earlier was a trade-mark of Paterson's art.

TWO TREES

SUBJECT

The 'Don Miguel' of the poem, it has been suggested, is a reference to the poet's friend, the New York poet Michael Donaghy, who died in 2004. After moving to London in 1985, he played with Don Paterson in the early line-up of the music group, Lammas. Don Miguel grafts an orange tree and a lemon tree together which are then split by a subsequent owner of the house. Both trees survive the tearing apart.

FORM: RHYMING COUPLETS

This poem has two stanzas, each with twelve lines of rhyming couplets. With its 'One morning' opening, it suggests the start of a simple fable or parable, except that it refuses to give any obvious moral at its conclusion.

COMMENT

Like Don Miguel, Paterson shows himself to be a master of his craft, with a fine balance between the two stanzas: the first deals with the grafting, the second with the severing. With its full rhymes and springy rhythm, it deals lightly, almost playfully, with closeness and separation. It talks in strictly unsentimental terms, for *trees are all this poem is about,* as Paterson tells us, *and trees don't weep or ache or shout.*

The first stanza deals with the painstaking craft of Don Miguel/Donaghy and the resulting abundant fruitfulness triggered by it (*each bough looked like it gave a double crop*) – so much so, that it was seen as *the magic tree.*

However, when the hybrid tree is split apart, Paterson uses a series of three very firm negatives to stress that the separated trees were physically undamaged and continued to grow as usual: *And, no they did not die [...] nor did their branches bear a sterile fruit [...] nor did their unhealed flanks weep every spring ...*

Yet, with the lines *each strained on its shackled root to face/ the other's empty, intricate embrace,* we are made aware of a profound sense of loss. Paterson turns his face against the poetic clichés often associated with separation: dying of a broken heart, the end of creativity, endless tears. Nevertheless, when he writes of the straining towards *the other's empty [...] embrace,* there is an unstated acknowledgement that, no matter how much the speaker insists (as Paterson does in public readings) that this is simply a poem about trees, the terrible pain of human severing can also be detected. Some view it as a graceful, unsentimental tribute to the loss of a friend.

THINGS TO DO AND THINK ABOUT

Although *11.00 Baldovan* and *Two Trees* both use couplets, they appear to be very different poems in terms of subject matter and tone. Consider the idea of loss and/or change in each poem. In what way does this idea make a link between the two poems? What is lost and/or changed in each one?

ONLINE

Key in 'Don Paterson Two Trees YouTube' into your browser and watch Don Paterson reading *Two Trees.*

DON'T FORGET

The six poems we are studying in this Guide differ greatly in terms of topics and techniques. In the final high-value question – worth half the marks of the full question – you will be asked to examine links between the given extract and at least one other poem. Make sure your notes are sufficiently full to be able to spot common elements such as a similar theme, character, imagery, form and setting.

ONLINE TEST

Want to revise your knowledge of this? Head to www.brightredbooks.net and take the test.

THE FERRYMAN'S ARMS AND NIL NIL

THE FERRYMAN'S ARMS

SUBJECT

An unidentified 'I' is waiting for a ferry in a pub called 'The Ferryman's Arms'. He takes himself on in a game of pool which he wins, naturally. The ferry arrives, the speaker boards it, reflecting on the part of himself that was *the losing opponent*. Paterson makes much use of the connotations of the notion of the ferry and the pub's name. Ferries bridge two sides of a divide: in Greek mythology, the living from the dead; here, Paterson explores this and the divisions in the human personality in considering this. The embrace implied in the pub's name suggests Paterson is in the grip of this contemplation.

FORM: FREE VERSE

The 30-line poem has two stanzas and is written in free verse. The first 20-line stanza describes the scene in the pool hall, and the second 10-line stanza is devoted to the ferry's arrival and the speaker's departure.

COMMENT

This is a poem that illustrates Don Paterson's fondness for finding depth in the everyday and using his wealth of cultural knowledge to make connections. On the one hand, we have the everyday in the shape of a pub called 'The Ferryman's Arms'; but its name also triggers an association in Paterson's mind with Charon, the ferryman in Greek mythology who ferried the souls of the dead across the Styx, the river separating the dead from the living. This grim association leads the speaker from a half-pint of Guinness and a game of pool in an eerily empty pub to an inspection of the divisions in his own inner self before he journeys towards a mysterious shoreline that is difficult to make out.

The reader is drawn into the poem by the enjambment of the first sentence covering the first four lines, much in the way the speaker is drawn, *magnetized* even, into *the darkened back room* where he has been attracted *like a moth,* (in mythology often a symbol of the soul seeking truth) by the *remote phosphorescence* towards the pool table. (And we remember, too, how fatal a flame can be to a moth ...)

Although the remark *I took myself on for the hell of it* is common enough, there are immediately other hellish connotations raised when he slots *a coin in the tongue.* At one level, this is the mechanism for releasing the pool table to users, but at another, it is also a reference to the custom in Greek mythology of placing a coin in the mouth of the deceased to pay the ferryman, Charon.

In addition, there seems a ghostly, vaguely human presence as balls are deposited *with an abrupt intestinal sound* and the striplight awakes *in its dusty green cowl*, like some hooded figure. (Charon is often depicted this way – or is it fate doling out personal destiny as *the balls were deposited*?)

The poem's central act is now under way: the self's confrontation with itself in a pool game, but also, metaphorically, a thoughtful exploration of *the darkened back room* of the dark recesses of the mind. The 'I' (or one side of it anyway) wins, thanks to *a rash of small miracles* making *an immaculate clearance,* despite the unpromising, dilapidated nature of the table. In this game of chance, fate appears to be on his side for the moment. Victory came when *the black/ did the vanishing trick.* This is an image triply rich in associations: obviously, it refers to the disappearing ball and the downed Guinness but also with the re-asserted presence of *the white* which rolls back *as if nothing happened*. This might be a hint that the speaker is moving away from darker, blacker thoughts, perhaps of death.

In stanza two, the ferry arrives *from somewhere unspeakable* (an unpronounceable local name or some hellish region of the mind?). Paterson combines his exit mechanisms from this moment: for example, the Guinness and the surrounding sea (which is *as black as my stout*), but he is still uncertain of his destination as his Guinness-flecked lip *mussitates endlessly* (*mussitate*: to talk indistinctly) with a *nutter's persistence* trying *to read and re-read the shoreline* – or, in other words, what awaits him. Although the winner embarks on the ferry, we are left with a stronger image of the loser, *stuck in his tent of light,* practising for a future confrontation between the two sides of the speaker's consciousness. Who, we wonder, will win next time?

NIL NIL

SUBJECT

At one level, the speaker charts *the fifty-year slide* of a football club from its zenith to Sunday League, to 'thirty-a-sides', to a boy kicking a pebble down a drain. The pebble turns out to be the gallstone of a fallen wartime pilot. At another level, its panorama of descent sees a pattern of connections in human life which spirals out to encompass the infinite.

contd

FORM: EPIGRAPH, FREE-VERSE NARRATIVE AND EPILOGUE

The poem begins with an epigraph from the *Pensées* of François Aussemain, a character and work totally of Paterson's invention, which helpfully sets out the poem's core idea: that of the continuing interconnectedness of all human experience, stretching out until it disappears into *a point so refined/ not even the angels could dance on it.*

The poem encompasses two free-verse narratives that might initially appear totally unconnected but meet, bizarrely, via a gallstone stuck in a drain-cover.

A six-line epilogue, in which the poet addresses the reader directly, concludes the poem.

COMMENT

In its mix of the everyday, the bizarrely surreal and its interest in the human condition the poem is epitomises Paterson's style embodying his comment that *poetry is a form of magic, because it tries to change the way we perceive the world....* For the poem's black humour and strange perspectives help colour our final view of the world depicted.

It begins ordinarily enough, as it jokingly shows us (punningly) *in silent footage* an early First division football team at its peak. The mock-heroic comic portrayal of *McGrandle, majestic in ankle-length shorts/his golden hair shorn to an open book* invites us into Paterson's humorously observed world: *a plague of grey bonnets* greets temporary success followed by the departure of key players *detaching/like bubbles to speed the descent into pitch-sharing.* We laugh at Paterson's witty description of decline: bottom of the Second division, Sunday League, Boys' Club, *unrefereed thirty-a-sides* until we are left with *two little boys* playing with *a bald tennis ball,* then only one, who finds what he thinks is a stone and gets it jammed into a drain-cover. The poem's repeated use of enjambment underlines the seemingly unstoppable slide into inglorious decline. This helter-skelter of descent further accelerates with Paterson's telling use of a welter of meticulously observed details which mark various landmarks of descent:

> *open hatchbacks parked squint behind goal-nets,*
> *the half-time Satsuma, the dog on the pitch.*
> *the Boys' Club, sponsored by Skelly Assurance*
> *then Skelly Dry Cleaners, then nobody;*

Our laughter at wee Horace Madden's antics is halted abruptly. The poem takes off in a surreal direction. We discover the 'stone' he is playing with is the gall-stone of a World War two fighter pilot, killed when his engine fails and he bails out only to find his parachute is the victim of an April Fool's Day prank. Here we have another chain of – literally- descending events as the pilot falls. There is an odd mixture of black humour and beauty as we watch

> *the ripcord unleashing a flurry of socks*
> *like a sackful of doves rendered up to the heavens*
> *in private irenicon.* (irenicon: a peace-making gesture)

Burnt to death, all that remains of the pilot is the gallstone which connects both narratives.

In its black humour, its delight in connecting the unlikely, in its eye for deftly observed detail, a relish for cultural allusions, (in this case, largely the culture of football – *the dismal nutmegs, absolute sitters, spectacular bicycle-kick-* but also for rarer ones from the world of religion- *irenicon-),* its concern with the human condition, this poem illustrates many hallmarks of Paterson's style.

THINGS TO DO AND THINK ABOUT

The Ferryman's Arms and *Nil Nil* are perhaps the most challenging poems of the six in terms of complex ideas. List the points you might make in a group discussion of how Paterson's use of poetic techniques helps make these ideas more understandable and approachable. Why not stage the discussion itself to clear up any lingering questions you may have about meaning?

 DON'T FORGET

In the exam, you will often be asked in the preliminary questions to analyse how a poet conveys a certain effect. This means pointing to specific words and phrases and then commenting on the particular effect they have. Make sure your notes are sufficiently specific and full to allow you to do this. Generalisations won't do!

ONLINE TEST

Head to www.brightredbooks.net and take the test on this section.

 VIDEO LINK

Watch Don Paterson reading some of his poetry at www.brightredbooks.net

ENGAGING WITH THE POEM

Now that you have studied all six poems and explored their ideas, structures and techniques, you are ready to look closely at one of them in the way you will have to do in the exam. As we've said before, you won't know which poem you will be examined on. Your teacher's comments, study notes and focused discussion in class will all help a great deal, but the best way to prepare is to study the poems in your own time, and get to know them really well.

Read the following poem, and then answer the questions that follow:

11.00 Baldovan

1   Base Camp. Horizontal sleet. Two small boys
     have raised the steel flag of the 20 terminus:

     me and Ross Mudie are going up the Hilltown
     for the first time ever on our own.

5   I'm weighing up spending power: the shillings,
     tanners, black pennies, florins with bald kings,

     the cold blazonry of the half-crown, threepenny bits
     like thick cogs, making them chank together in my pockets.

     I plan to buy comics,
10   sweeties, and magic tricks.

     However, I am obscurely worried as usual,
     over matters of procedure, the protocol of travel,

     and keep asking Ross the same questions:
     where should we sit, when to pull the bell, even

15   if we have enough money for the fare,
     whispering, Are ye sure? Are you sure?

     I cannot know the little good it will do me;
     the bus will let us down in another country

     with the wrong streets that suddenly forget
20   their names at crossroads or in building-sites

     and where no one will have heard of the sweets we ask for
     and the man will shake the coins from our fists onto the counter

     and call for his wife to come through, come through and see this
     and if we ever make it home again, the bus

25   will draw into the charred wreck of itself
     and will enter the land at the point we left off

     only our voices sound funny and all the houses are gone
     and the rain tastes like kelly and black waves fold in

     very slowly at the foot of Macalpine Road
30   and our sisters and mothers are fifty years dead.

THINGS TO DO AND THINK ABOUT

Read through the extract above thoroughly before reading and attempting the following questions:

1   Evaluate the effectiveness of lines 1–8 in creating a vivid sense of anticipation.   **4**

2   By referring closely to lines 9–16, analyse how Paterson achieves a change of identity from the small boy contemplating the worries of the journey to the adult looking back on his younger self.   **2**

3   In lines 17–30, the poet reveals the growing distress of the speaker. Analyse how the poet conveys the speaker's state of mind.   **4**

4   By referring to this poem and at least one other by Paterson, discuss how he can use a commonplace or apparently superficial event to say something much more profound.   **10**

 DON'T FORGET

Do not spend too much time on the earlier questions and leave yourself short of time for the final question with its 10 marks.

GUIDANCE ON POSSIBLE RESPONSES

POSSIBLE RESPONSES TO QUESTION 1

1   Evaluate the effectiveness of lines 1–8 in creating a vivid sense of anticipation.

Refer to any two of the following:

- *Base Camp. Horizontal sleet.*: these brief phrases set out as sentences give the impression of a mountaineer's log/diary entry as he anticipates the climb ahead. What will the climb bring?

- *For the first time ever on our own*: the fact they are totally unsupervised and making an unprecedented trip which they clearly view as a journey into the unknown adds to the anticipation of what they will encounter.

- *I'm weighing up spending power*: by taking stock of their financial situation, the speaker is clearly involved in and preparing for what the future may bring as they embark on their adventure.

POSSIBLE RESPONSES TO QUESTION 2

2   By referring closely to lines 9–16, analyse how Paterson achieves a change of identity from the small boy contemplating the worries of the journey to the adult looking back on his younger self.

The language/word choice/vocabulary Paterson employs distinguishes the boy from the reflective adult:

... obscurely worried [...] over matters of procedure, the protocol of travel: suggest the terms used by an educated adult when they are concerned. (1)

Refer to any one of the following:

- *keep asking the same questions*: suggests the repetitive behaviour of a small boy in doubt. (1)

The series of questions about seating arrangements, leaving the bus and having sufficient money are the worries of a small boy tackling a journey of this kind for the first time rather than those of an adult. (1)

- *Are ye sure? Are you sure?* The fact that he is so insecure about travelling arrangements that he has to ask very basic questions more than once suggests the behaviour of a small boy. (1)

POSSIBLE RESPONSES TO QUESTION 3

3   In lines 17–30, the poet reveals the growing distress of the speaker. Analyse how the poet conveys the speaker's state of mind.

Refer to any two of the following:

●   Enjambment: from line 18 to the end of the poem is one long breathless sentence as the speaker's worries and fears flow ever faster and become ever more serious. His panic builds to a climax until it ends on the word *dead*, and a sense of ultimate dread.

●   The repetition of the word *and* six times in its key position as the first word in the line suggests that the speaker sees one fear piling on top the next one in an ever-mounting list of terrors.

●   The repetition of the word *will* shows the certainty in his own panic-stricken mind of the terrible fates surely awaiting them: *the bus will let us down … no one will have heard of the sweets…*

●   The scenes he imagines become increasingly terrifying in the futuristic nightmare they depict: *the charred wreck* of the bus; *our voices sound funny; black waves* wash into Macalpine Road; their mothers and sisters are *fifty years dead.*

POSSIBLE RESPONSES TO QUESTION 4

4   By referring to this poem and at least one other by Paterson, discuss how he can use a commonplace or apparently superficial event to say something much more profound.

Possible responses could include the following:

Nil Nil: a football match leads on to a discussion of the interconnected nature of all existence; it also leads on to a connection with and some thoughts on death (of the pilot). Here the death is not an imagined one as in *11.00 Baldovan.*

The Thread: a father playing 'aeroplanes' with his boys leads him to reflect on how close one of the boys came to death at his birth.

The Ferryman's Arms: a half-pint of Guinness and a pool match with himself leads the speaker to question the nature of personality.

You can obtain a further 2 marks by discussing how the commonplace (in this particular extract, a local bus trip) can lead to a consideration of the real and disturbing terrors lurking in some young people's minds.

You can obtain 6 more marks by discussing in some detail how the commonplace can lead to a consideration of a deeper truth about the human condition in the other poem(s) you have selected. A relevant reference to a technique/idea/feature will give you one mark, and an appropriate comment will give you another mark. If you do this three times, you have your 6 marks. Or you could also obtain 6 marks by giving two references and a more **detailed/insightful** comment. Quality of comment rather than quantity of references is what to aim for here.

 THINGS TO DO AND THINK ABOUT

Remember that there is never any one 'correct' response to these questions. But, when you see 4 marks for a question, think in terms of giving two full responses – each one giving a specific reference followed by a detailed/insightful comment about the text.

 **DON'T FORGET**

Ask your teacher to check your responses and to give you a steer on your own self-evaluation.

CRITICAL ESSAY WRITING: MAXIMISING PERFORMANCE

WHAT AM I BEING ASKED TO DO?

The good news is that you know quite a lot about writing critical essays already. Think for a moment about your preparation for Reading for Understanding, Analysis and Evaluation. The skills you are learning for answering detailed questions in this paper form a solid basis for writing critical essays, too. Your essay needs to:

- show understanding
- show analysis
- show evaluation
- express your ideas well.

SHOWING UNDERSTANDING

Your knowledge of the text (or texts) needs to demonstrate that you are totally secure in discussing what is going on in it. You need to know the characters in depth, what motivates them, how they behave, how they change, how they interact with others and what other characters think of them. You need to know the main themes that bind the text together. You also need to be familiar with setting and how it might change from time to time and perhaps alter the mood of the text.

SHOWING ANALYSIS

In terms of showing analysis, you are well prepared for the critical essay, because you've already have experience of producing evidence to back up your understanding in Reading for Understanding, Analysis and Evaluation. You already know about figurative language (such as similes and metaphors), sentence structure and tone. You already know how to select appropriate quotations or refer to key incidents or events to back up your case.

SHOWING EVALUATION

This is your opportunity to give your own opinion about what the writer has been saying, how they have been saying it and how effectively you think they have been saying it. Think about the points you made in your analysis, base your evaluation on specific details that you have identified, then take them a little further by giving your personal opinion about them.

DON'T FORGET

No matter how good your teacher, you are not going to arrive at the standard necessary if you leave learning your text (or texts) until the last minute. Read your text regularly in your own time so you can get to know it in detail.

EXPRESSING YOUR IDEAS WELL

This means not only writing clearly and accurately with the correct spelling, grammar and punctuation, but also being able to structure your essay persuasively by framing it with a relevant introduction and conclusion, by following a clear line of argument throughout and by using critical terminology to set out your thoughts in the most convincing way possible.

We'll deal with this one step at a time as we work through this chapter.

ORGANISING A STUDY FILE

Prepare yourself for the critical essay question at the start of the course. Get yourself a study file that you update regularly. Decide how best you memorise information, and organise your notes and quotations in a way that works for you. For example, if you are studying a play, you could organise your notes by what happens in acts and scenes, by understanding characters and their changing fortunes throughout acts and scenes or by themes.

If you are studying a novel, you could keep a chapter-by-chapter summary, a page for each of the characters and their changing fortunes or organise your notes by themes.

If you are studying a short story or poem, go through the same process.

Store all your class work, weekly essays and notes in this file, and it will become an invaluable revision tool.

REGULAR REVISION

You are being asked to work with detailed and complex texts, so it's a good idea to read your notes at least once a week. That way, you'll get to know the text really well, deal with any questions as they arise and avoid major problems and panics at exam time. And that can only be good for your confidence.

THE CHALLENGE OF THE QUESTION

Conscientious students often emerge from the examination room with a strong sense of frustration. They feel they have studied and revised well and have only been invited to demonstrate a fraction of their acquired knowledge. But answering an exam question well is a process of selection. The examiners do not wish to know everything your teacher has taught you. They are more interested in focusing on one question and finding out how well you can select the information required to answer it.

 ## THINGS TO DO AND THINK ABOUT

Leave one page of your study file free so you can make notes about possible exam angles. For example, what themes are emerging in your play: ambition, jealousy, greed or intolerance?

What kinds of characters are you meeting: a strong woman, an indecisive character, a young person, someone who changes?

What is the setting: a city, countryside, the past?

In other words, what directions could you imagine a question coming at you from? A good way to speculate about possibilities is to organise a group discussion. You can never guess what might be in the examiner's mind. But saying aloud what you think a text light be seen to be *about* could be helpful in defining your view of the text. And finding out what *others* might think it might be about could be a handy revision tool for deepening your text-specific knowledge. You might find your ideas change as you get deeper into the text.

 ONLINE

Check out the SQA's guide to Critical Essay Writing at www.brightredbooks.net

 ONLINE TEST

How well have you learned this topic? Take the test at www.brightredbooks.net

SELECTING THE QUESTION

WHAT DO I NEED TO CONSIDER HERE?

Choosing the correct question is vital. You only have 45 minutes to answer the question, so you'll need to decide quite quickly how your knowledge dovetails with the question. And, to do that, you have to be confident that you know your text really well. Once you have decided that you have enough information to settle on a question, begin by checking the wording carefully and underlining or highlighting what you think are key words or phrases.

Example

Suppose you came across a question like this:

> Choose a poem which explores an experience in childhood or adolescence or old age.
>
> Discuss how the poet's presentation of this experience adds to your understanding of the central concern(s) of the poem.

What speedy mental checks do you need to make?

Step 1: Have you studied a poem about any of these stages of life? Suppose you had studied *Death of a Naturalist* by Seamus Heaney. This is a poem that begins by describing a boy catching tadpoles but ends up saying much more about childhood and growing up. So, yes – this poem would be a good match to the question.

Step 2: What are the key words in the question? What does *explore an experience* mean? Well, looking in detail at the framework of the experience is surely important: who undergoes it, what happens, where does it happen, when does it happen and what is the effect on the boy? Do you have a sufficiently clear understanding of the experience to answer the question?

Step 3: The words *discuss how the poet's presentation* should alert you to the fact that you are going to have to talk about figurative language, characterisation, setting and structure. Do you have enough detailed knowledge of the language to produce quotations to back up the point you are making?

Step 4: *adds to your understanding* means you are going to have to engage with the poem and say what you learned about – in this case – the discovery of guilt and the pain of growing up. Can you evaluate how the experience has added to your understanding of the 'central concern(s)' of the poem?

If you have gone through these steps and answered all these questions confidently, you are well on track for a successful essay. Double-check that you have looked at **all** the key words in the question and not simply the first ones you come to.

DON'T FORGET

Selecting a question involves a thorough check of the wording throughout the question. Once you've done that, check that your in-depth textual knowledge is sufficient to answer the *entire* wording of the question.

HOW ABOUT QUESTIONS ON PLAYS AND PROSE WORKS?

Questions on plays, novels and short stories require a similar approach, although, in a prose work or play, analysis can take the form of discussing key incidents or events in considerable detail. But quotations are also vital if you wish to convince the examiner that you have a secure knowledge of the text. A good essay will be rich in both forms of evidence.

ONLINE

To hear and see Seamus Heaney reading *Death of a Naturalist*, head to www.brightredbooks.net

ANALYSING THE QUESTION

Before we start thinking about the plan, we need to look at the poem itself.

DEATH OF A NATURALIST BY SEAMUS HEANEY

The speaker – a young boy – visits a disused flax-dam *in the townland* (which is the smallest unit of land division in the Irish administrative system). Flax was used in the making of linen and had to be stored under water to avoid drying out. It is a hot day in this country setting, and the boy relishes the feel, smell and sound of every aspect of

contd

the scene while he gathers frogspawn, as he has done for several years. He shows this proudly to his primary teacher, Miss Walls, who uses it for a rudimentary lesson on reproduction and weather forecasting.

But, when he goes on a second visit, he comes across adult frogs making a terrifying noise, and he runs away, terrified, thinking they have come to get their revenge on him for stealing their frogspawn – hence the 'death' of his interest in being a naturalist.

Let's go through the process we identified above and match up the information we have with the wording of the question.

'explores an experience'	We need to outline the two sides of the experience: the pure delight the boy took in gathering frogspawn at the flax-dam until the out-and-out terror drove him to abandon the place and the activity. For the experience to be appreciated fully, we need to give some idea of the boy undergoing this experience and how it affected him.
'discuss how the poet's presentation'	Poem (and experience) presented in two scenes. Free verse. Use of a variety of poetic techniques (onomatopoeia, alliteration, assonance etc.) to convey atmosphere of both moments.
'adds to your understanding'	The boy's experience adds to our awareness of how a young person comes to realise that actions have consequences, and that this loss of innocence can cause great pain. Heaney's words work on us in the way the experience worked on the boy.

Death of a Naturalist by Seamus Heaney

All year the flax-dam festered in the heart
Of the townland; green and heavy headed
Flax had rotted there, weighted down by huge sods.
Daily it sweltered in the punishing sun.
Bubbles gargled delicately, bluebottles
Wove a strong gauze of sound around the smell.
There were dragon-flies, spotted butterflies,
But best of all was the warm thick slobber
Of frogspawn that grew like clotted water
In the shade of the banks. Here, every spring
I would fill jampotfuls of the jellied
Specks to range on window-sills at home,
On shelves at school, and wait and watch until
The fattening dots burst into nimble-
Swimming tadpoles. Miss Walls would tell us how
The daddy frog was called a bullfrog
And how he croaked and how the mammy frog
Laid hundreds of little eggs and this was
Frogspawn. You could tell the weather by frogs too
For they were yellow in the sun and brown
In rain.
Then one hot day when fields were rank
With cowdung in the grass the angry frogs
Invaded the flax-dam; I ducked through hedges
To a coarse croaking that I had not heard
Before. The air was thick with a bass chorus.
Right down the dam gross-bellied frogs were cocked
On sods; their loose necks pulsed like sails. Some hopped:
The slap and plop were obscene threats. Some sat
Poised like mud grenades, their blunt heads farting.
I sickened, turned, and ran. The great slime kings
Were gathered there for vengeance and I knew
That if I dipped my hand the spawn would clutch it.

 ## THINGS TO DO AND THINK ABOUT

Now apply the same process to a play, short story or novel **you** have been reading. Mark up key words and create a grid of your own in which you outline how your information will match up with the wording of the question. If the question above doesn't suit, choose one of the following:

Choose a play in which a central character feels isolated from family or social life around him/her. Explain the reasons why the character feels this way, and discuss how the playwright's presentation of his/her circumstances adds to your understanding of the play as a whole.

Choose a novel or short story which deals with a social or political or religious issue. Discuss how the issue is explored and how its presentation enhanced your appreciation of the text as a whole.

 ### DON'T FORGET

Remember that this is **not** a plan. It is basically a mental process that you can go through before you get down to the plan itself. It will become second nature with practice. Use it whenever you are given a trial essay.

 ### ONLINE TEST

Head to www.brightredbooks.net and take the test on this section.

PLANNING A RESPONSE

ONLINE

For an idea on how plans can be approached, check out 'Exam essay writing: planning and getting started under time pressure' at www.brightredbooks.net

ONLINE

Create your own mind-map online. Go to www. brightredbooks.net

DON'T FORGET

The ideas and quotations in your mind-map are your first thoughts. As you progress into your essay, you might decide to change or get rid of some of them for various reasons. Don't worry! It shows you are thinking like a professional writer. But an initial plan is a must for a clearly focused argument.

THE IMPORTANCE OF PLANNING

Time is of the essence in an exam. You have already used up some of your 45 minutes by selecting a question and considering a possible response. But the worst thing you can do is let the pressure get to you and start writing without a plan.

Without a plan to refer back to from time to time, you risk going off-task. As a result, you can lose your line of argument and end up not answering the question. Consequently, you do not make the best use of your knowledge – or gain your best possible mark.

For the marker, too, plans are vital. A planned essay is instantly recognisable from the moment of reading the introduction. It follows a clear line of argument from start to finish; it is not a random collection of intelligent comments. Markers appreciate – and reward – an essay with internal coherence, and this only happens with structured planning.

Everyone has their own way of planning an essay. Some make lists of points under various headings such as setting, characterisation, relations with others and techniques. Others like to draw mind-maps, like the one opposite.

Here are some ideas for a plan to answer a question on a childhood experience, using *Death of a Naturalist*.

ORDERING THE PLAN

Now we know what we want to say, we need to decide how we're going to organise our information. The position of the introduction and conclusion is a given, but what's the best way to arrange the key points of our essay?

AVOID THE GUIDED TOUR

Avoid the 'guided tour' approach to essay writing. This means trying to answer the question by following the sequence of events presented by the text, fitting your answer to the order in which things happen in it. This order suited the writer, but it does not necessarily mean it will suit you as you try to answer the question. Some re-organisation of information could well lead to a more persuasive essay. This applies to plays and prose works just as much as poems. Do not be nervous about doing this.

ESTABLISH THE SPEAKER/CENTRAL CHARACTER

When we're discussing an 'experience', it makes sense to identify the person who undergoes that experience. In this case, it's a boy. We get some key information about him from line 11: he likes to collect frogspawn, he believes his teacher unquestioningly, and we infer from his *mammy/daddy* vocabulary that he is of primary-school age. This information is hinted at earlier in his reaction to the flax-dam, but only confirmed here.

EXPLORE THE EXPERIENCE

Our next two points will deal logically with the sequence of events that make up the 'experience' – in this poem, the 'death' of the naturalist: the delight in the pastime and its later abandonment.

REMEMBER THE WORDING OF THE QUESTION

The next step is to discuss how this presentation 'adds to your understanding of the central concern(s) of the poem'. This is the penultimate paragraph, before the conclusion. Remember not to leave this discussion until the end of your essay, because you might run out of time. It's better to finish each paragraph by making it clear how what you have just discussed has added to or advanced your understanding of the 'central concern(s)' of

contd

the writer. When you come to the penultimate discussion paragraph, you can extend this discussion more fully.

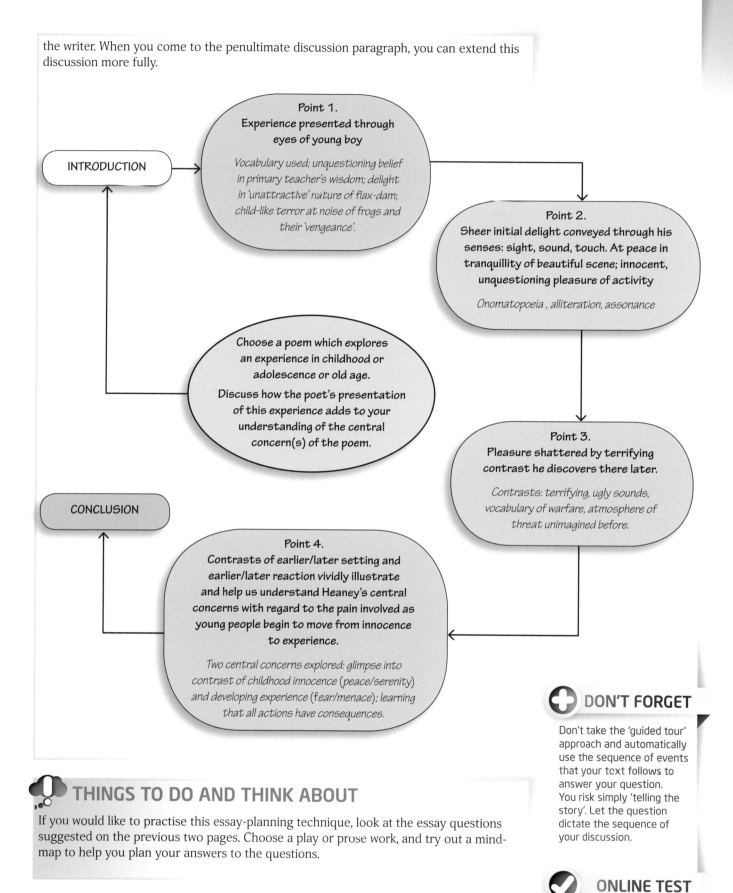

INTRODUCTION

Point 1.
Experience presented through eyes of young boy

Vocabulary used; unquestioning belief in primary teacher's wisdom; delight in 'unattractive' nature of flax-dam; child-like terror at noise of frogs and their 'vengeance'.

Point 2.
Sheer initial delight conveyed through his senses: sight, sound, touch. At peace in tranquillity of beautiful scene; innocent, unquestioning pleasure of activity

Onomatopoeia , alliteration, assonance

Choose a poem which explores an experience in childhood or adolescence or old age.

Discuss how the poet's presentation of this experience adds to your understanding of the central concern(s) of the poem.

Point 3.
Pleasure shattered by terrifying contrast he discovers there later.

Contrasts: terrifying, ugly sounds, vocabulary of warfare, atmosphere of threat unimagined before.

CONCLUSION

Point 4.
Contrasts of earlier/later setting and earlier/later reaction vividly illustrate and help us understand Heaney's central concerns with regard to the pain involved as young people begin to move from innocence to experience.

Two central concerns explored: glimpse into contrast of childhood innocence (peace/serenity) and developing experience (fear/menace); learning that all actions have consequences.

THINGS TO DO AND THINK ABOUT

If you would like to practise this essay-planning technique, look at the essay questions suggested on the previous two pages. Choose a play or prose work, and try out a mind-map to help you plan your answers to the questions.

DON'T FORGET

Don't take the 'guided tour' approach and automatically use the sequence of events that your text follows to answer your question. You risk simply 'telling the story'. Let the question dictate the sequence of your discussion.

ONLINE TEST

Want to revise your knowledge of this? Head to www.brightredbooks.net and take the test.

STARTING TO WRITE 1

Now that you've got a plan, you have established the broad outline of your essay. The next thing to do is to write an effective introduction that leads into the body paragraphs of your essay.

INTRODUCTIONS: MAKING A GOOD FIRST IMPRESSION

A good introduction immediately suggests to the marker that you have planned your answers intelligently and that your knowledge of the text is thorough. It will also give them a favourable first impression that will probably influence them when they mark the rest of the essay. Here's a checklist for a successful introduction:

1 State the title of the selected text (in inverted commas!) and its author clearly in your first sentence.

2 In the same sentence, adopt some wording which suggests that you have chosen this text because it fits the set question.

Let's consider our earlier *Death of a Naturalist* question:

> **Choose a poem which explores an experience in childhood or adolescence or old age.**
>
> **Discuss how the poet's presentation of this experience adds to your understanding of the central concern(s) of the poem.**

You could cover steps 1 and 2 by recycling some wording from the question to give:

A poem which explores an experience of childhood is 'Death of a Naturalist' by Seamus Heaney.

Follow this with a very brief summary – no more than 4 or 5 lines – of what happens in the poem:

In this intriguingly entitled poem, Heaney describes how a young boy delights in visiting a disused flax-dam to gather frogspawn to present to his teacher. One day, however, he is terrified to hear the angry croaking of frogs. Seriously troubled, he interprets their arrival as signalling a desire for revenge for his theft of their eggs, thus leading to the 'death' of his interest in this pastime.

Now re-visit the wording of the second part of the question to assure the examiner you have not forgotten about that second part:

Heaney's presentation of the boy, his delight and his terror are helpful in making clear his interest in showing how a child moves from innocence to experience, and how painful this transition can be.

Note that, in this example, we are giving not just a reference **back** to the question but also a reference **forward** to our 'road-plan' for the essay: discussion of the boy, his experiences and what insight it brings to our understanding of child development.

Your introduction is your first opportunity to impress the examiner. You'll do this if you signal clearly and concisely what the structure of your essay is going to be.

DON'T FORGET

If you find your plot summary is going on for much more than four or five lines, there is something terribly wrong with it. Stop immediately. Give just enough information to make sense of the poem's outline. You need time to construct your case, not to re-tell the story.

VIDEO LINK

For more on writing a great introduction, check out the clip at www.brightredbooks.net

BODY PARAGRAPHS: MAKING YOUR CASE

We jotted down four key points in our plan. These will form the basis for the opening statement(s) of each paragraph in the core of our essay, whether on poetry, prose or drama.

STATEMENTS SHOW UNDERSTANDING

Our plan overleaf listed clear points.

> Point 1. Experience presented through eyes of young boy.
>
> Point 2. Sheer initial delight conveyed through his senses: sight, sound, touch. At peace in tranquillity of beautiful scene; innocent, unquestioning pleasure of activity.
>
> Point 3. Pleasure shattered by terrifying contrast he discovers there later.
>
> Point 4. Contrasts of earlier/later setting and earlier/later reaction vividly illustrate and help us understand Heaney's central concerns with regard to the pain involved as young people begin to move from innocence to experience.

Now we need to develop these key points into something more than points; they need to be transformed into statements. Each statement forms the opening of your body paragraph and outlines the line of thought each body paragraph will establish. Each statement can run to more than one sentence since it needs to be sufficiently substantial to prepare the way clearly for the evidence you will shortly be giving. Above all, opening statements must each make clear your *understanding* of a major point in your essay. If you list them one under another these statements will give an idea of your essay in miniature.

Here's an example:

> **Statement 1:** To help us understand fully the central concerns of this poem, Heaney goes to some lengths to make readers aware that the experience is being presented from the perspective of a young boy. His age is never given but, from clues planted in the text, we infer he is of primary-school age.

> **Statement 2:** Although there are aspects of the description of the flax-dam that might not appear so attractive to adults, they do not trouble the boy, who clearly delights in the location. He is serenely happy as he goes about collecting his frogspawn, with Heaney conveying his happiness through the sensual pleasure the boy takes in the scene.

> **Statement 3:** At some point later, the boy re-visits the flax-dam, but this time the atmosphere could not be more different. Gone is the tranquillity as he hears the loud, angry croaking of adult frogs. His vivid imagination pictures them being there to seek revenge for his treatment of their young. With this comes a dawning realisation of guilt for his past behaviour.

> **Statement 4:** The boy's reaction is such that, as the poem's title tells us, it leads to the 'death' of his interest in nature. The contrasts depicted in the poem are there to help us understand why this 'death' took place and to give us an insight into Heaney's central concerns in telling us about this. This experience has begun to teach the boy some of the painful lessons that all young people learn as they begin to develop a moral sense.

 DON'T FORGET

A good statement section sets out the agenda for the rest of the paragraph. Don't be nervous about letting it run to more than one sentence. The statements show the marker your secure understanding of what is going on in the text.

 DON'T FORGET

A good statement section should not give away too much detail. Give away your detail here and you will be stuck for things to say in the next section, which backs up your statements with evidence.

 ## THINGS TO DO AND THINK ABOUT

Take one of the texts you are studying at the moment, and try to summarise it in the way you might do in an exam question. Better still, look back at the questions on page 77, choose one and try to write a full introduction to your answer.

 ONLINE TEST

How well have you learned this topic? Take the test at www.brightredbooks.net

STARTING TO WRITE 2

Now that you have the opening statements for each paragraph, you need the **evidence** to back up the facts laid out in your statements. In other words, as in your analysis answers for Reading for Understanding, Analysis and Evaluation, you need evidence from the text to give conviction to what you have just claimed in your statements.

EVIDENCE: SUPPORTING YOUR STATEMENTS

Evidence can take two forms: direct quotations from the text or detailed references to information in the text. A good essay will make use of both. In poetry answers, it is usual for most of your evidence to come from direct quotations.

Let's try this out. First, look back at the poem and at the opening statements on page 77. Now we're going to add evidence to lead on from opening statement 1:

> To help us understand fully the central concerns of this poem, Heaney goes to some lengths to make readers aware the experience is being presented from the perspective of a young boy. His age is never given but, from clues planted in the text, we infer he is of primary-school age. **This is suggested by his word choice in referring to 'the daddy frog' and 'the mammy frog' and her 'little eggs'. The fact that he also accepts unquestioningly the dubious weather-forecasting skills attributed to frogs by 'Miss Walls' (that frogs turn yellow in the sun and brown in the rain) suggests the kind of belief in teachers' wisdom held only by very young children. He is also fairly typical of small boys in actually seeming to enjoy the fact that the flax-dam 'festered' in the heat, not minding the fact that 'it sweltered in the punishing sun', and finding 'the warm thick slobber' of the frogspawn 'best of all'.**

DON'T FORGET

Evidence in a critical essay can take the form either of quotations or detailed references to information in the text. If you are writing about a poem, use quotations as your evidence.

So, we have now produced sufficient evidence to back up the claim in our statement section that this is a scene viewed from the perspective of a small boy. But our body paragraph is far from complete. We need to produce a commentary on what the reader is to make of our statements and evidence. It would also be a good idea to try to tie in a link to the 'central concern(s)' reference in the question, so let's pass on to the next stage of our body paragraph.

COMMENTARY: CLINCHING YOUR CASE

After providing your statements and accompanying evidence, we need to go a little further and suggest to the marker what all this points to. In other words, you need to unpack the evidence a little and show how it establishes the point(s) you are trying to make. You need to **evaluate** its significance for the reader. So, how do you go about this?

THE USEFULNESS OF THE LEAD-IN PHRASE

To help your paragraph flow smoothly, you will need a number of lead-in phrases to move the reader from the evidence to your commentary, phrases such as:

From evidence such as this, we can see that ...   *From this we may understand that ...*
Clearly, then, ...   *Alert readers will note that ...*
This suggests that ...

Let's see how such phrases can help you with a commentary on our statements and evidence so far. Continuing from finding 'the warm thick slobber' of the frogspawn 'best of all', we might write:

> Clearly then, Heaney has gone to some trouble to establish the fact that the crisis to come will be experienced by a child young enough to believe that frogs may actually have come to take revenge on him for his frogspawn-collecting.

contd

Given that a central concern of the poem, as we shall begin to see later, is presenting the dawning of guilt and responsibility in the mind of the boy, his earlier innocence and unthinking attitude need to be made clear quickly.

And there your paragraph is complete! Note that, as well as explaining in our commentary the significance of our evidence to our statements, we have touched also on the 'central concern(s)' mentioned in the initial question, to reassure the marker that we are already dealing with it and will be coming back to discuss it again later.

You have made a **Statement** setting out the identity of the boy (showing **Understanding** of the text).	S
You have produced **Evidence** to back up this point (showing **Analysis** of the means by which you came to this understanding).	E
You have helped the reader with an explanation of what all this evidence is suggesting by providing a **Commentary** on it all (showing an **Evaluation** of the evidence's implications).	C

Using this SEC format will help you keep your paragraphs on track in a way that showcases your knowledge to best advantage. It also gives the examiner a clear pathway to follow your arguments along.

CONCLUSIONS: ROUNDING OFF WELL

Don't let the pressure of time in the exam room put you off attempting a conclusion that rounds off convincingly the arguments you have been putting forward in the previous paragraphs. It doesn't need to be all that long, but it does need to perform certain tasks to secure your standing as a credible commentator on literature. Here are a few guidelines:

1   The first sentence of this concluding paragraph should refer back to some wording of the question itself. Here you are reminding the marker you have kept to the original task: *Standing back from the text as a whole, we see that Heaney* **has presented the experience in such a way that he has added imaginative depth to our understanding** *of what it is to ...* Note there is also an opening phrase which signals you are rounding off the essay.

2   You should go on to sum up **briefly** the main points you have been making in the central section of your essay.

3   On no account bring in new points or quotations at this late stage. It will only spoil the sharp focus of the case you have been making throughout your essay.

4   In the introduction, you said what you were going to say; in the conclusion you are really saying what you have said in summary form – just to remind the marker of what your initial intentions were. A good tip here is to have a number of synonyms up your sleeve for key words. It will add variety by avoiding verbal repetition.

5   Try to leave time for a conclusion – however short – otherwise your essay will simply stop rather than arrive at a convincing note of finality.

 THINGS TO DO AND THINK ABOUT

The skills that helped you make sense of Reading for Understanding, Analysis and Evaluation questions – the ability to understand (shown in your **Statement**), analyse (shown in your **Evidence**) and evaluate (shown in your **Commentary**) – can also help you to structure persuasive critical essays. The SEC structure is the building block of the body paragraphs of critical essays, so remember it and use it.

It will help your critical essay-writing skills greatly if you take some aspect of the play, poetry or prose work you are studying and write a single SEC paragraph of about 250 words on it. Not only will it get you used to the technique – it will also give you a more detailed understanding of the text. Here are some ideas to get you started:

The importance of setting in a scene, poem or prose work	How a character is established in a novel or short story
Why the opening/closing scene of a play is effective	Why a particular episode is significant in a novel or short story
How a writer makes an unattractive character interesting	How a writer arouses pity for a particular character

 **DON'T FORGET**

If you find structuring an essay paragraph quite challenging, you might find this method quite useful and helpful. Or you might have your own way or doing this. Choose what works best for you. Just remember that however you construct your paragraph, it must have a clearly-argued central point and be backed up by textual evidence that you discuss in your own way with the reader.

 DON'T FORGET

Statement
SAY IT
Evidence
SHOW IT
Commentary
SELL IT

 ONLINE TEST

Head to www.brightredbooks.net and take the test on this section.

VIDEO LINK

For more on this, watch the clip at www.brightredbooks.net

MAINTAINING THE FLOW

Talk to markers, and they will tell you that the most successful critical essays follow a clear line of thought from start to finish. Readers should not be brutally jerked from one topic to another and somehow expected to see a link between them. You should give some serious thought about how to link topic to topic, paragraph to paragraph and how to signal an upcoming conclusion. There are a number of signalling words, phrases and techniques that will help you achieve this.

ONLINE

You'll discover some of the simpler signalling words at www.brightredbooks.net. You'll already use many of these to change direction, sequence events or illustrate your points. Familiarise yourself with the whole range available to you. Once you have done this, look at how the longer phrases we discuss below can also help you improve the flow of your writing.

DON'T FORGET

If you practise writing effective linking statements, you will dramatically improve your writing style and, therefore, your performance in the exam.

FROM INTRODUCTION TO FIRST PARAGRAPH

It's a sensible idea to introduce a 'road-map' approach to the last lines of your introduction by indicating what you'll be covering in your essay. For example, your introduction might end with the words 'Donovan arouses sympathy for the protagonist through her handling of Miss O'Halloran's social isolation, the use of symbolism and second person narrative.'

Make sure that you then go on to cover these three topics (her social isolation, the use of symbolism and the second-person narrative) **in the order mentioned** here, beginning the first SEC paragraph after the introduction with phrases such as:

Examining first Miss O'Halloran's social isolation, we notice that …

Isolated socially, Miss O'Halloran has only …

The social isolation of Miss O'Halloran is insisted on by Donovan throughout the short story.

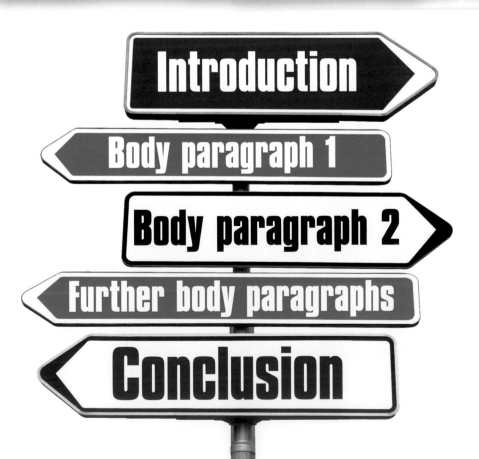

FROM ONE BODY PARAGRAPH TO THE NEXT

Once you have completed the discussion of your first point, you now have to lead the reader smoothly onto the next point. In this example, you must therefore lead the reader from your paragraph about Miss O'Halloran's 'social isolation' to a paragraph that discusses the 'use of symbolism' in the story – the second area you mention in your road-map. You can do this effectively by using statements like these:

> The sympathy aroused by the old lady's social isolation is further intensified by Donovan's use of symbolism.
>
> Equally effective in arousing our sympathy for Miss O'Halloran is the way Donovan uses symbolism.
>
> Symbolism is the second technique by which Donovan invokes our sympathy for her protagonist.

Successful flow is ensured by making a brief reference – direct or indirect – in the first sentence of your new paragraph to the subject of your previous paragraph.

Then you need to complete the process until you come to the conclusion.

INDICATING A CONCLUSION

Your essay's flow should be neatly rounded off by signalling that the final stages are approaching with a 'summing up' phrase, followed by a reminder of what was said in the introduction.

> Seen overall, this is a short story in which the author successfully employs the techniques of ... to bring us close to the misery of ...
>
> Standing back, we note that throughout the tale the techniques mentioned in the introduction have succeeded in ...
>
> Summing up, we have seen that the three techniques of ... have been successfully employed to arouse our sympathy for a character who ...

By using these opening phrases, you are signalling clearly that you are writing a conclusion, and that you are summarising the points you raised in your introduction. In this way, you will round your essay off in a thoroughly satisfactory manner.

THINGS TO DO AND THINK ABOUT

Before testing out these suggested guidelines by writing a new essay, try this experiment with a partner:

Take an essay that you have already written, and adapt the techniques and phrases we have suggested here to lead smoothly from introduction to first paragraph, from paragraph to paragraph and then into the conclusion. You don't need to re-write the whole essay, just the linking sentences. Now read these linking sentences aloud to a partner. You will notice that you have added real authority to your writing.

DON'T FORGET

All of these sentences would make suitable statements which you could develop successfully to create a convincing SEC paragraph.

ONLINE

Read this *Guardian* article online: 'A sea of red that evokes thoughts of more than just algae' at www.brightredbooks.net. You'll see how the first statement of each paragraph links to what has come before. This gives it a smooth flow and makes it easier to read. The same should be true in your critical essay writing.

DON'T FORGET

Writing a strong introduction, followed by persuasive well-formed body paragraphs, is crucial if you want to succeed in your critical essay. However, a smooth flow from paragraph to paragraph is equally important. It helps the reader understand that there is continuity in your thought – and throughout your essay.

ONLINE TEST

Want to revise your knowledge of this? Head to www.brightredbooks.net and take the test.

PERFECTING YOUR PERFORMANCE

You are now in a position to create a successful critical essay. Here are some ways that you can turn it an excellent critical essay.

USING QUOTATIONS TO BEST EFFECT

LONGER QUOTATIONS

There is more than one way to introduce a long quotation to your paragraph.

Sometimes you will pave the way for a quotation by first describing it. In this case, you should use a colon (:), drop a line, indent slightly and begin the quotation using inverted commas, for example:

Her clear-sighted sadness is seen in the words:

'I have betrayed a great man and his like will never be seen again.'

Sometimes your sentence will not describe the quotation, but simply introduce it. In this case, the colon would only interrupt the natural flow of the words. So, instead, you should write:

Her clear-sighted sadness is seen when comments that she has

'betrayed a great man and his like will never be seen again.'

Always make sure your longer quotations have room to breathe; drop a line (with or without a colon), indent slightly and add quotation marks. Drop another line before continuing your own text.

SHORTER QUOTATIONS

A good essay will have a mixture of longer and shorter quotations. Shorter ones can be just as effective as longer ones. If you can't remember the full quotation, you can use the parts you remember to great effect.

For example, if you wanted to use the following quotation:

'the street shone out in contrast to its dingy neighbourhood, like a fire in a forest'

but you couldn't quite remember it in full, you could use the phrases you do remember to good effect and paraphrase the rest:

The street is described as making a sharp contrast to its 'dingy neighbourhood' and standing out 'like a fire in a forest'.

As long as you weave the short quotations seamlessly into your own text, this kind of paraphrase-plus-quotation will prove more effective than a longer, misquoted extract. It could also pinpoint more sharply the exact point you wish to make.

GIVING A CONTEXT

Never assume that readers understand more than they do. No quotation, however well chosen, will have its desired effect unless you give it a brief **context**. In other words, indicate briefly not just who said it, but why and under what circumstances it was said. If, for instance, you had been reading *Macbeth* and wanted to make a comment about King Duncan's generosity of nature, you might want to mention his kindness to a wounded messenger – but be careful how you do it.

contd

DON'T FORGET

If you can't remember the exact wording of the extract you want to quote in your essay, a series of short quotes will serve you just as well – if not better!

ONLINE

For a more detailed review of how to use quotations correctly in your essay, read 'The Writer's Handbook: using literary quotations' at www.brightredbooks.net

Duncan shows he has a great generosity of nature:

> 'Go get him surgeons.'

Duncan has a great generosity of nature. Seeing a badly-wounded messenger collapse, he personally orders him to be taken care of:

> 'Go get him surgeons.'

A context does not need to be long; it simply needs to lead readers into the quotation in a way that helps them make sense of the point you are making.

WRITING AN EFFECTIVE LEAD-IN

Make sure your lead-in to the quotation does not simply repeat the content of the quotation. For example, in this description about *Buddha Da* by Anne Donovan, a bad lead-in would be:

> Jimmy tells his wife he is going on a journey but he is not sure where he is going:
>
> 'Ah'm on a journey but ah don't know where ah'm gaun.'

A better lead-in would be:

> Jimmy comes across to his wife – and to readers – as rather vague about his plans for taking his study of Buddhism forward:
>
> 'Ah'm on a journey but ah don't know where ah'm gaun.'

In other words, a thoughtful lead-in does more than simply help the reader to understand the quotation's context; it can also underline your ability to evaluate its significance.

ONLINE TEST

How well have you learned this topic? Take the test at www.brightredbooks.net

THINGS TO DO AND THINK ABOUT

It's an accumulation of factors that will achieve you a top mark. Here are some of the key ones. Study them well before you enter the exam room.

- You need to demonstrate a thorough knowledge of your texts. That means reading them not just in class but regularly on your own as well.
- You must select **only** the information from your text knowledge that answers the specific question in front of you. Examiners do not want to know everything your teacher has taught you.
- You must be alert to all sections of the question and apportion your time accordingly.
- You need a plan that is more than just a loose collection of good points to help you structure a coherent essay. There should be a line of argument that the examiner can follow easily as one paragraph flows smoothly into the next.
- Each paragraph should be carefully structured to ensure that your claims are borne out by evidence and that you unpack this evidence for the reader.
- When a question has a second part to it inviting you to discuss 'central concerns' or to expand on how some aspect 'enhances your understanding of the text as a whole' or to comment on 'how it engages your interest in a portrayal', don't leave it all until the penultimate paragraph to discuss fully. You could leave yourself short of time. Instead, keep this discussion in sight by referring to it in each paragraph. You can then expand on it in the penultimate paragraph.
- A soundly structured introduction will help you to stay on task, and a 'road-map' in the introduction's last sentence will help the marker to find their way round your arguments. A brief conclusion will remind them of your key points.
- Use the correct procedure for laying out quotations, long or short. This shows good academic manners and attention to detail that increases your stature as a competent commentator on your texts.
- Make sure your quotations make sense. That means checking that you have given each one a context, however brief.

TRYING OUT YOUR ESSAY SKILLS

Now it's time to put all these skills into practice.

 **ACTIVITY:** COMPLETING THE ESSAY

Below, you will find **one** possibility for the start of the essay that we have been working on in this chapter. Use the knowledge you have acquired to complete the missing sections. The introduction and first SEC paragraph have been completed for you. If you are having any problems, revisit the various sections in this chapter to remind yourself of what constitutes a fully persuasive SEC body paragraph and conclusion.

> **Choose a poem which explores an experience in childhood or adolescence or old age.**
>
> **Discuss how the poet's presentation of this experience adds to your understanding of the central concern(s) of the poem.**

A poem which explores an experience of childhood is 'Death of a Naturalist' by Seamus Heaney. In this intriguingly entitled poem, Heaney describes how a young boy delights in visiting a disused flax-dam to gather frogspawn to present to his teacher. One day, however, he is terrified to hear the angry croaking of frogs. Seriously troubled, he interprets their arrival as signalling their desire for revenge for his theft of their eggs, thus leading to the 'death' of his interest in this pastime. Heaney's presentation of the boy, his delight and his terror are helpful in making clear his interest in showing how a child moves from innocence to experience and how painful this transition can be.

To help us understand fully the central concerns of this poem, Heaney goes to some lengths to make readers aware the experience is being presented from the perspective of a young boy. His age is never given but, from clues planted in the text, we infer he is of primary-school age. This is suggested by his word choice in referring to 'the daddy frog' and 'the mammy frog' and her 'little eggs'. The fact that he also accepts unquestioningly the dubious weather-forecasting skills attributed to frogs by 'Miss Walls' (that frogs turn yellow in the sun and brown in the rain) suggests the belief in teachers' wisdom held only by very young children. He is also fairly typical of small boys in actually seeming to enjoy the fact that the flax-dam 'festered' in the heat, not minding the fact that 'it sweltered in the punishing sun', and finding 'the warm thick slobber' of the frogspawn 'best of all'.

Now complete this paragraph giving evidence drawn from the poem and a comment of your own on this evidence.

> *Although there are aspects of the description of the flax-dam which might not appear so attractive to adults, they do not trouble the boy, who clearly delights in the location. He is serenely happy as he goes about collecting his frogspawn, with Heaney conveying his happiness through the sensual pleasure the boy takes in the scene.*
>
> _____
>
> _____
>
> _____
>
> _____

contd

Now complete this paragraph giving evidence drawn from the poem and a comment of your own on this evidence.

At some point later, the boy re-visits the flax-dam, but this time the atmosphere could not be more different. Gone is the tranquillity as he hears now the loud, angry croaking of adult frogs. His vivid imagination pictures them as there to seek revenge for his treatment of their young. With this comes a dawning realisation of guilt for his past behaviour.

_____

_____

_____

_____

Now complete this paragraph giving evidence drawn from the poem and a comment of your own on this evidence.

The boy's reaction is such that, as the poem's title tells us, it leads to the 'death' of his interest in nature. The contrasts depicted in the poem are there to help us understand why this 'death' took place and to give us an insight into Heaney's central concerns in telling us about this. This experience has begun to teach the boy some of the painful lessons that all young people learn as they begin to develop a moral sense.

_____

_____

_____

_____

Now have a go at completing the conclusion of the essay.

Standing back from the text as a whole, we see that Heaney has presented the experience in such a way that he has added imaginative depth to our understanding of two central concerns of his here: that taking responsibility for our actions is part of the growing-up process and it is, as the boy discovers, a painful experience. The realisation is expressed in contrasting pictorial and aural imagery which allows us to share in the boy's changing states of mind, from delight to terror, and, through this process, to identify with his anguish.

_____

_____

_____

_____

 THINGS TO DO AND THINK ABOUT

Remember that there is no single way to write a good essay. Everyone's opinion is valid and valued – provided your statements are matched by convincing evidence and comment. There is a suggestion for a completed essay online, at www.brightredbooks.net. This isn't the **only** way to tackle such an exercise, but it provides a practical working model for answering exam questions of this kind.

PORTFOLIO WRITING: REACHING A HIGHER LEVEL

THE PORTFOLIO: SHOWCASING YOUR SKILLS

With the portfolio you are presenting for CfE Higher English, you are showcasing the writing skills you have been acquiring since you began school. Your performance here has to be seen at its very best if you are to do justice to more than ten years' hard work by you and your teachers.

Before you even begin to think about committing anything to paper, you need to reflect on how to show off your skills to maximum advantage. And, although you don't need to present the portfolio until well into the course, start thinking now about genre-selection and how best to polish your skills for whatever genre you finally choose.

ONLINE

Check out some quality journalism online at www.brightredbooks.net or any of the other major broadsheet websites.

DON'T FORGET

Copying is plagiarism. But adopting ideas or techniques from writers who impress you and adapting their approach to your own work is, in fact, how many professional writers learn their trade.

READ THE BEST

In your Higher year, there are lots of demands from other subjects on your reading time. Try to think of your Higher English reading as a welcome escape from the pressures of your other work: quality writing of all kinds including novels, short stories, biographies, travel writing and the best journalism is always a pleasure to read. It's also one of the best ways to improve your own writing: you can learn a lot from professional writers.

You can source good reading material by asking staff in quality bookshops and libraries for their recommendations. Investigate quality journals and newspapers online.

Look out for techniques that you can adapt and use in your own writing. For example, you could be inspired by the gripping start to a story, the bringing to life of a character or setting or dialogue that crackles with realism and apply it to your own creative and reflective writing. Or you could learn from an engagingly witty opening to an opinion piece or a well-written illustrative example and apply what you have absorbed to add authority to your discursive texts. There is no shortage of models out there to study. Adopt a few ideas from the professionals, adapt them to suit your purpose and your writing will progress.

MAKE EXISTING KNOWLEDGE WORK FOR YOU

You can also improve your writing by using some of the very techniques that you've been analysing in your Reading for Understanding, Analysis and Evaluation texts. Think about using minor sentences, inversion, figurative language, word choice and parallel structures in your own work. We'll look at this further on in the chapter.

BEFORE YOU START...

WHY AM I WRITING ABOUT THIS?

Don't waste time by writing about something that doesn't interest you. If it doesn't, you'll end up with something you decide to scrap or, worse, something mediocre. If you need to ask yourself why you are writing about your chosen topic, then it's not the right topic to write about.

WHAT DO I KNOW ABOUT THIS?

Professional writers will always tell you their best work comes from writing about what they really know about. Write from your existing life experience or knowledge base, or about a topic you really want to get to know about. For example, the court of Louis XIV

contd

is ruled out as a setting for a short story – unless you really want to do serious research. Your family, your friends, your life experience – these are all rich veins of material to be mined. Discursive writing will always need research, so you must be prepared to roll up your sleeves to get the most reliable, up-to-the-minute information. But keep to areas that interest you.

WHAT IS MY PLAN?

Your work on critical essays should already have taught you that important essays – and these are about the most important you have written so far – must have a soundly structured plan. Use whatever method works for you, whether it's a mind-map, a listing of possibilities or a brain-storming page. Tinker with the plan until you get your thoughts organised into a logical sequence of paragraphs.

IS THIS A GOOD PLAN?

As you write, you might find that weaknesses show up in your plan, or that you suddenly think of a better idea as you become more familiar with your subject. Don't worry about this. Professional writers will tell you this happens to them, too. Don't be scared to move paragraphs about, delete sentences, add phrases, discard a word to find a better one or do whatever seems sensible. Technology makes all this possible. Try out various ideas before you finalise your thoughts.

FOR WHOM AM I WRITING?

Only professional writers have the luxury of writing to please themselves. By all means, enjoy your writing process, but remember there is a marker lurking out there. Try to keep that in mind. Crisp, clear, structured prose that offers a rich reading experience will impress, whatever the genre. Some good ideas or catchy phrases that are cobbled together will not.

WHAT IS MY PURPOSE?

You need to reflect carefully on the aim of your chosen genre. Are you seeking to persuade, analyse, entertain or inform? Whatever your ultimate objective, you must keep checking your writing to make sure that it is fulfilling that objective. For example, maybe you started out to be persuasive but then you slipped into informing mode instead. Maybe when you look back at your short story it's merely a sequence of facts rather than a text with a developed use of characterisation and setting to advance your plot. Keep checking that your language is appropriate for the task you set yourself.

CAN I DO BETTER?

No matter how good your short story or your analysis of the shortcomings of capitalism, it won't get a good grade unless you pay attention to basics. Before handing in any draft, proofread it to check the grammar, spelling, punctuation and vocabulary choice. Don't get caught out with basics like *its/it's, there/their, to/too* and the like. Mistakes like these say a lot about you in a piece of writing of this importance – and what they say is not good …

 THINGS TO DO AND THINK ABOUT

Start making preparations for your two folio pieces long before the deadline. For example, start a programme of reading in areas that interest you, and that you would like to explore further. Read for enjoyment, but notice how professional writers tackle things like realistic dialogue, gripping starts, witty similes and varied sentence structure. You can learn a lot from them.

 ONLINE TEST

Want to revise your knowledge of this? Head to www.brightredbooks.net and take the test.

WHAT AM I GOING TO WRITE?

You are expected to write two portfolio pieces of up to 1300 words each, which will account for 30 per cent of your final grade. If you are not always at your best in exams, this is a chance to make a major difference to your grade, so think carefully about the topics that you choose.

WHAT ARE THE CHOICES?

One of your two pieces will be drawn from the genres identified in Group A, the other from Group B. The possibilities are as follows:

Group A: broadly creative

- a personal essay
- a reflective essay
- an imaginative piece

Group B: broadly discursive

- an argumentative essay
- a persuasive essay
- a report for a specified purpose

Before making any decisions about your choices, let's take a look at two popular genres in each group to see what each one involves. That way, you'll have a better idea about which ones best match up to your skills.

ONLINE

For some advice about writing short stories, visit 'Your Story Club: How to write short stories – 10 tips with examples by our chief editor' at www.brightredbooks.net

GROUP A: CREATIVE

Imaginative Fiction	Personal/Reflective
If you have done well so far in writing short stories or fiction generally, this is a really pleasurable choice. The best stories do not need to be peppered by dramatic events: in some of the best ones, very little happens, but attitudes, moods and reflections allow scope for study. If you are not already sure if prose fiction is something you enjoy, a portfolio piece for an important exam probably isn't the best place to find out.	At Higher level, markers will be looking for depth to your ideas. Choose a topic that permits serious reflection. Nobody can write better about you or your ideas than you yourself. You already have the information to hand; it's just a question of digging deep to bring the experience and reflections alive for others.
Opportunities	**Opportunities**
Within the word limit, you are free to create your own world. Here you are free to conjure up atmospheric settings, characters who become convincingly alive, dialogue that fully reflects the characters and their life-styles. Their fates are all in your gift. You must be prepared to explore all the possibilities of figurative language in the way of a professional writer.	This needs to have all the same power to create a rich reading experience as an imaginative piece. The techniques of successful imaginative writing should be explored. The difference here is that you are not creating an imaginary world, it's one in which you live yourself, a world in which your narrative and reflections are anchored in your own reality and experience.
Considerations	**Considerations**
At Higher level, an imaginative piece needs to be much more than a yarn. It needs depth in behaviour and character analysis. Remember that setting can also assist in your narrative. Remember, too, the need for a strong sense of structure. You will find the word limit imposes restrictions on any unnecessary introductions. Here a plan is very necessary before you begin. Feel free to alter it, but never lose sight of the overall shape. Limit your characters if they are to be described fully. Remember that contrasting characters will spark conflict, which is great for moving stories on.	You need to choose your material really well. It must have sufficient depth for you to reflect on it and on any lessons it taught you. Discovering you had a talent you had not previously suspected will provide this depth; a day out to a safari park probably will not. Reflecting on some incident from your past could allow you to discuss how time has given you a new perspective on the event/experience.

GROUP B: DISCURSIVE

Argumentative/Persuasive	Report Writing
At Higher level, you are in a very strong position to write successfully in either of these genres. Your studies in other subjects such as History or Modern Studies have armed you with plenty of factual material to get you started. If you have a strong interest in a topic, enjoy researching for information, organising your findings in a convincing way and presenting them with authority, then this might be a sensible choice for you.	A report is written to gather together factual, researched information. It is often produced prior to decision-taking by someone other than the writer. The information has to be precise and it must be easily assimilated. If you are a practical person, this choice might suit you very well. This is certainly not the arena for demonstrating your imaginative writing skills.
Opportunities	**Opportunities**
Here you can explore your chosen topic in two ways: you can try to persuade others to share your viewpoint on an issue, or you can debate two sides of topic by laying out the facts of a case in a logically organised structure. The essential thing is to enjoy researching and sharing your results in prose which reads fluently and carries real conviction.	You can usefully carry this kind of writing over into the world of work, since it requires a 'real world' mindset to be successful. You are attempting to convey information in a way that will help the reader to understand the realities and practicalities of a situation. Your prose needs to guide the reader clearly through factual material of various kinds.
Considerations	**Considerations**
Getting the tone correct for whatever discursive option you select is of key importance here. Persuasive writing requires you to adopt an outgoing, emotive approach; argumentative debating or factual report writing require you to adopt a much more neutral tone. Which of these approaches best suits you? Remember, too, the best discursive writing needs research to convince, but facts cannot be allowed to substitute for clearly presented viewpoints of your own.	Your information needs to be as carefully researched as it would be in a persuasive or argumentative essay. Since practical considerations are also concerned – for example, the transmission of information or the communication of advice/warnings – there can be no overlooking of factual detail vital to the successful completion of the task. Your prose, formal in tone, needs to be totally at the service of the information to be communicated.

 DON'T FORGET

Don't finally commit yourself to any essay choice until you are sure that you know enough about the topic, or are really keen to learn about it.

 DON'T FORGET

Start to try out ideas and plans well before the deadline; be prepared to accept that your first thoughts might not be your best ones. Successful portfolio writing is about being willing to draft and redraft several times before you even think about presenting a first version to your teacher.

 ONLINE TEST

Head to www.brightredbooks.net and take the test on this section.

THINGS TO DO AND THINK ABOUT

Before you commit yourself to any genre, take a look back at past work you have produced in English. Your teachers' comments and marks should give you a good idea of where your strengths and weaknesses lie. Think, too, about which of these pieces you felt were the most successful, or which ones you enjoyed writing most. These could provide pointers to future choices.

WRITING CREATIVELY

WRITING SHORT STORIES

There are three pillars for writing prose fiction that you should always keep in mind: character, setting and plot. Sometimes students are so focused on plot that character and setting tend to get forgotten. All three need to be kept alive throughout, because characters who do not come alive but simply remain names on a page fail to engage the reader's interest, and narratives that take place in a vacuum create little in the way of atmosphere to catch the reader's attention.

Remember, too, that while a good essay can be achieved in less than 1300 words, the maximum you can write is only 1300 words. That means you have to set certain limitations on your narrative. Do not be too ambitious in your cast of characters or the timescale of your narrative. Remember this when you set about your planning.

SO, HOW DO I PLAN A SHORT STORY?

A practical way to start might be to set yourself a series of 'who, what, where, when, why and how?' tasks that you can tackle in any order you wish, depending on how you like to compose fiction. Here are a few suggestions about how to get started.

Where?	• Setting is a key factor in a good short story. A detailed, realistic setting is a good place to start a fiction piece. But remember to keep this going with brief references to it as the story progresses. We'll talk about some of the things you can do with setting later.
	• To write well about setting, you need to know it intimately. Use your first-hand knowledge: your street, the shops you go to, your town.
	• Given your word limit, don't change setting too often, or you'll use up too many words. But you can always refresh it – for example, the re-appearance of the same street, but at night.
	• Think of films you have enjoyed where the setting transported you to a setting that felt totally real. Your narrative should do the same. It should transport readers to a place of your invention and **keep** them there.
Who?	• Your word limit means you need to restrict your characters to a number you can describe adequately. Don't introduce characters who play little part in the final outcome. Two, three or four might be a sensible cast list.
	• Contrasting characters often lead to conflict, which moves a story along very nicely. For example, try contrasting youth and age, rich and poor, sensible and rash, shy and outspoken or good-natured and quick-tempered.
	• Jot down facts about each character before you start. Not just appearance, but personality traits, nervous habits, likes, dislikes, hobbies, interests, tastes in music, people, food ... Don't blurt these all out at once but weave them from time to time into your narrative. Passing references to such features bring characters alive.
What?	• Again, your word limit reduces the kind of story you can handle here. Epic adventures are out. To be successful, a good short narrative need not be about dramatic events; a minor incident carefully observed and imaginatively related is more likely to suit the required length of your text. Time sequences of hours, days or weeks are probably more practical than years or decades as your time frame.
When?	• The present causes less trouble, but if you have an interest in earlier periods, some basic research might furnish a credibly different setting, while a fertile imagination could provide the detail necessary to convince in a sci-fi tale.
	• Remember that setting encompasses not only a place and period but the seasons, weather and time of day as well. These can be manipulated tellingly to bring atmospheric colour to your fiction. Use them to reflect changing moods and attitudes of your characters in their situations. For example, spring/green/shoots/hope or evening/mist/threat.

contd

Why?	• Credibility is something you need to be alert to. So, why something happens needs to be addressed carefully. The far-fetched can weaken even the most carefully realised settings and characters. Keep the plot within the bounds of the believable. At Higher level, you really need to be demonstrating a fairly adult attitude to credibility; the far-fetched creaks badly and makes markers groan.
How?	• Think about how the story is to be told. Is the narrator to be 'I'? This will bring you close to the speaker and his/her thoughts. Or are you going to use the third-person narrator: he or she? This will let you observe everyone and allow you into everyone's thought-processes. • And how is the plot to advance? In normal time sequence or by a dramatic flash-forward or flash-back? These latter two will get you off to a flying start before you go back and fill in the details. Many successful films use this technique.

BUT WHAT IF I FIND PLOTS DIFFICULT?

Have a look at the following useful plot-creating structure:

> A settled situation involving a minimum of characters (perhaps two or three).

> A complication deriving from something happening: a letter arriving, an accident, a serious illness, a new character appearing or the loss of someone or something.

> An increase in tension due to the new situation.

> A crisis leading to a turning point in the affairs of all concerned.

> An ending with a perceived change in how matters stand compared with how they stood at the beginning. Perhaps the unhappy are now happier, perhaps a relationship has altered – for the better or the worse – or perhaps characters simply have changed their view of themselves or of someone else. Or perhaps as readers we have changed our perception of a character or situation.

You'll probably be able to think of many good short stories that use only some of these features, or perhaps none at all. A good short story can take many forms, provided it has sufficient elements of character, setting and plot to create an enjoyable reading experience. So, don't be tied down by this suggestion. You might find elements of it useful – dip in and out of them and use whatever helps you to get started.

 THINGS TO DO AND THINK ABOUT

Your school or college library will have no shortage of anthologies of short stories. Try to find time to browse through a few short stories to see how professionals give shape to their material. *Beggar's Banquet* by Ian Rankin is a good collection. Look in particular at *A Deep Hole* and *Trip Trap* – there is a perceived change that occurs in each of these short stories.

 **DON'T FORGET**

Remember that while 1300 words might seem a lot, you'll probably find that you use them up rather quickly. So, be ruthless with elements that do not add meaningfully to the characterisation, plot or setting you have set yourself. Keep your drafts on your computer so you can edit out word-limit-threatening detail. Don't make final deletions until your final draft: you might find some other use for your out-takes.

 ONLINE TEST

How well have you learned this topic? Take the test at www.brightredbooks.net

 ONLINE

Wanting some inspiration for a starting point? Head to www.brightredbooks.net

PUTTING SETTING TO WORK

Earlier, when talking about the 'where' and 'when' of your story, we suggested that setting should not just be mentioned at the start of your story and then forgotten about. By coming back to it from time to time and maybe viewing it under different conditions, you can help flesh out what your characters are feeling or undergoing at any particular point.

Here we will look at how two major Scottish writers weave setting into their texts.

IAIN BANKS

This is Iain Banks in *The Crow Road* describing a country landscape:

> The rain fell with the impression of gentle remorselessness west-coast rain sometimes appears to possess when it has already been raining for some days and might well go on raining for several more. It dissolved the sky-line, obliterated the view of the distant trees, and continually roughened the flat surface of the loch with a thousand tiny impacts each moment, every spreading circle intersecting, interfering and disappearing in the noise and clutter of their successors.

We are not surprised to learn that the characters suffering from this rain are in fairly glum mood: the rain, as part of the setting, is helping tell the story, and things are not going well.

 **ACTIVITY** LET'S TRY THAT OUT

Try experimenting with setting yourself. As a writer, think what you would do with the description of that loch when:

- it was being visited by a young couple very much in love and enjoying a perfect day out. What would you do to the appearance of the loch and its surroundings to match the mood of the moment?

- it was being visited by a young couple who had just had a terrible argument which probably spells the end of their romance. What would you do to the appearance of the loch and the accompanying weather to match the mood of the moment?

Try writing a paragraph of description for each moment. The idea is to back up in the setting what the characters are going through. In other words, how can weather and surroundings reinforce the plot-line of your story?

IAN RANKIN

Here, Ian Rankin describes a street scene in the short story *Trip Trap*:

> Gillan Drive was part of an anonymous working-class district on the south-eastern outskirts of Edinburgh. The district had fallen on hard times, but there was still the smell of pride in the air. Gardens were kept tidy, the tiny lawns clipped like army haircuts, and the cars parked tight against the kerbs were old – W and X registrations predominated – but polished, showing no sign of rust. Rebus took it all in in a moment.

All here looks to be perfectly in order, but the description of the spruce exterior does not tell the whole story.

ACTIVITY: LET'S TRY THAT OUT

The writer has established the street's setting in some detail to give us a feel for the area. Using what you have been told about the general appearance of the place, how would you as a writer present a house that:

- stood out from its neighbours, and hinted at something violent about its residents? What would you do to its appearance?

- stood out from its neighbours, and hinted at something unhappy about its residents? What would you do to its appearance?

Try writing your own paragraph, following on from the leads that Ian Rankin gives you.

From your own writing, you can see how setting can enrich your storytelling greatly. Remember that you don't need to write huge amounts of description: a few details can tell a great deal about characters and their mood or situation.

SETTING IS MORE THAN PLACE

Sometimes students get the impression that setting is about place: a street, a house, a night club. While this is true, it's also about much more than that, and can be realised in many other ways:

Time of day	Just as words have connotations, so, too, do times of day. Morning can be associated with a new beginning or fresh hope. Evening may suggest the end of things in some way. Night can be threatening. There are various possibilities to be had from working with your own associations of these times of day. One idea might be to have your story move through these times of day to underline various points in your characters' moods or situations.
Season	Again, seasons tend to carry connotations with them: spring, hope; summer, ripeness; autumn, harvest and the hint of an ending; winter, cold and death of the year. Of course, you might want to turn these connotations completely on their head to create contrasts: sadness in spring when everything else feels full of life, for example. Think of moving your story through a season or two.
Weather	We have already worked on matching weather to mood with our exercise on the Banks text. Weather is a powerful way of supporting the atmosphere you are creating around your characters. For instance, when something is starting to go wrong in a good relationship, maybe there is a rumble of distant summer thunder?
Objects	Something simple like a vase of flowers can add greatly to your storytelling. Fresh flowers; a few petals scattered on a table top; withered blooms in a dry vase: all these can signal landmark moments in an evolving narrative.

 ## THINGS TO DO AND THINK ABOUT

Here are fragments of text that suggest elements of setting which could be woven into your narrative to show evolving emotions/moods/situations. What story could these fragments tell? You could use this either as the basis of a discussion or, better still, try your hand at the story itself. Order the fragments in whatever order you like to underline developments in the narrative.

Lifting the vase of withered blooms off the window-sill, Pam wearily pressed their brown, decayed stems and leaves into the waste-bin, closing it firmly on them.

Opening David's note, she idly picked up the falling pink rose petals the evening breeze was scattering over the table.

Looking out of the hospital window, he saw the night closing in. He glanced at the clock. Still only five o'clock and yet it was dark already.

In the sharp noon light, the trees were etched sharply against the clear sky. The year was creeping on. He glanced at his Rolex. He was late.

The heavy scent of the full-blossomed roses filled the room with their heady perfume as she carefully arranged them in her mother's best crystal vase.

The gold of crocuses dotted the greening turf. He was careful to avoid stepping on them. Nature looked good today. Really good.

DON'T FORGET

Setting is not something to be mentioned once in the opening paragraph and then forgotten about. Keep refreshing it from time to time by reintroducing it at key moments, perhaps altered in some way, to underline the emotions/mood/situation that your characters are experiencing. Flowers wither; rain goes off; the sun goes in; changes happen. Record them. This will add a powerful dimension to your narrative that markers will notice.

 ### ONLINE TEST

Want to revise your knowledge of this? Head to www.brightredbooks.net and take the test.

 ### ONLINE

To get some extra inspiration for a setting for your story, head to www.brightredbooks.net

CREATING CONVINCING CHARACTERS

Unless your characters come alive for readers, you are always going to struggle to sustain interest in them. They don't always need to be likeable, but they do have to be interesting and, above all, convincing. So, how do we go about creating credible characters in imaginative writing? There are quite a number of ways. Let's take a look at some of the techniques we could employ here to bring characters alive.

EXPLORING THE SURFACE AND BENEATH

Perhaps the first thing we all expect from a fictional character is a physical description. Good writers, however, will often give you more than just a description. Built into their physical description is a hint of what kind of personality lies beneath the surface. Now, given the fact that we have only 1300 words at the very outside to create our fictional world, this is doubly useful: we can say what characters look like and hint at the inner person at the same time.

DON'T FORGET

Don't feel you have to write 1300 words in your folio pieces. Many excellent pieces are achieved in fewer than 1300 words. But you need to respect that limit.

Example

Look for a moment at how Donna Leon presents two of her characters in *The Anonymous Venetian* (Pan Books, London, 1995):

> Professore Ratti might have been in his early fifties, but he was keeping that fact at bay to the best of his ability. He was aided in the attempt by the ministrations of a barber who cut his hair so close to the scalp that the grey would be mistaken for blond. A Gianni Versace suit in dove-grey silk added to the youthful look, as did the burgundy silk shirt which he wore open at the throat. Someone once must have warned about the tendency of the skin to wattle, for he wore a knotted white silk cravat and held the chin artificially high, as if compensating for a careless optician who had put the lenses in his bifocals in the wrong places. (p. 261)

If we examine this pen portrait carefully, we see that character revelation is mixed in with physical description. Leon uses the first sentence as statement about the vanity of the man and his attempts to look young. Then she produces evidence which describes the man's physical appearance but which also gives an insight into personality. Now she turns to his wife:

> If the professor was fighting a holding action against age, his wife was engaged in open combat. Her hair bore an uncanny resemblance to the colour of her husband's shirt, and her face had the tautness that came only from the vibrancy of youth or the skill of surgeons. Blade-thin, she wore a white linen suit with a jacket left open to display an emerald-green silk shirt. Seeing them, Brunetti wondered how they managed to walk around in this heat and still look fresh and cool. The coolest part of them was their eyes.

We may not like this pair, but we certainly feel we know them, thanks to the extended metaphor of warfare that links their joint battle against ageing, the precise details about their hair and clothes and the final short sentence about the coldness in their eyes.

ACTIVITY LET'S TRY THAT OUT

Read over again Leon's portraits, noting how she mixes the surface and the inner person. Now try a similar approach to character realisation by selecting one of these:

- someone you know well (young or old) who always aims to be trendy
- someone you know well (old or young) whom you do not quite trust.

Keep in mind the usefulness of sentence structure (note the power of Leon's last, brief sentence), imagery, tone, parallel structures (*the vibrancy of youth or the skill of surgeons*). There is a lot to be learned here.

contd

SHOW AS WELL AS TELL

You can also reveal a great deal about your characters through their actions as well as their appearance and speech. Personality can be conveyed when you show them engaged in some really quite slight action: for example, the tapping of a foot, the snapping of a finger, the tidying of a room, the checking of a watch or yawning ostentatiously.

Example: An Obsessively Tidy Person

'Excuse the mess, please,' Claire said absently, wiping an already spotless coffee table with a Kleenex she produced from nowhere. 'Make yourself comfortable,' she added, plumping up a cushion and brushing an imaginary dog hair from the sofa. Raymond looked round the clinically tidy room and felt that being comfortable might interfere with Claire's austere seating arrangements. 'This room is in a right old state. What must you think of me?' she said apologetically. What indeed, Raymond wondered.

Here, we're shown as much as told what Claire is like; we are prepared for what turn her behaviour might take later in the story. How might difficulties arise between her and Raymond? Over what? Her actions define her as much as what she actually says.

Short bursts of description targeted at actions can often trigger ideas for a story. Try out a few. If you like what you write, you might consider a short story around this.

Try bringing one or two of the following people alive through a short action or series of actions:

- a vain person
- an aggressive person
- an affectionate person
- a greedy person

YOU ARE WHAT YOU SPEAK

Dialogue in fiction can often be seen simply as a means to move on a scene or situation, but it can also be another aid to successful character creation. Speech habits can tell you a lot about someone's personality. **How** people speak to each other gives you as much insight into them as **what** they actually say.

Use of sentence structure, word choice or use of dialect can often be key components in establishing the speech habits – and personality – of a character.

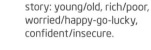 **ACTIVITY** LET'S TRY THAT OUT

Below are two character types. Examine the original speech of each character: how would you describe their personalities? What are their defining speech habits? Send them off on their allotted tasks, keeping their dialogue 'in character' in the way they talk in the scene. Invent speech characteristics for the person they talk to. If this works for you, could this be a basis for a short story?

	Personality? Speech characteristics?	Task
It's a job where ... how shall I put it? ... Where you need, you know ... to be, well, just a bit ... a bit ... decisive. Mm ... Yes, quite ... decisive.		Send this man off with his wife to Marks & Spencers to buy summer clothes for going on holiday to Italy. Keep his speech in character. Think about a contrasting speech habit for his wife.
Now, then. Let's see. Jake, you alright taking the girls? I'll follow in the Range Rover. Shall we meet up in Carlisle? It'll take about an hour. Right. Off we go!		This man has got himself into a minor car accident, with his Range Rover ending up in a ditch. Keep his dialogue in character as he tries to deal with the driver of the recovery lorry, who is a really dour, stubborn Scot.

 ## THINGS TO DO AND THINK ABOUT

Appearances, actions, speech habits, taste in clothes, music, cars: they all play their part in giving your characters life. As you would do with setting, keep reminding readers of aspects of their personalities as the story advances.

DON'T FORGET

A sharp contrast of characters will often lead to conflict. And conflict is effective in moving on a story. Think about pairs of opposing personalities who might work in your story: young/old, rich/poor, worried/happy-go-lucky, confident/insecure.

DON'T FORGET

Mixing Scots and Standard English-speaking characters can often give you a contrasting texture of languages and personalities. Or perhaps a Scottish character switches from Standard English to Scots at various times, for various reasons?

DON'T FORGET

Sometimes the comments of one character about another help define **both** characters. Imagine how a wicked character might dislike and despise a decent person for acts of kindness.

ONLINE TEST

Head to www.brightredbooks.net and take the test on this section.

ONLINE

For more on creating convincing characters, head to www.brightredbooks.net

BEING REFLECTIVE

WHY CHOOSE A PERSONAL OR REFLECTIVE ESSAY?

Nobody knows more about your life, your feelings, your experiences than you do. In writing either a reflective essay or a personal essay, you are drawing on resources unique to you. The writing process in either genre should bring out your hidden self and draw the reader into that very personal world.

Although grounded in your own lived experience, your writing here has to demonstrate all the sparkle of imaginative writing. That means drawing on the techniques that make imaginative writing pleasurable such as figurative language, varied sentence structure and carefully observed setting. Overall structure and planning are important here, too: your reflective or personal essay won't work if it's a loose rag-bag of thoughts, events and experiences.

DON'T FORGET

Don't be so absorbed in accurately expressing your reflections that you overlook the need for a rich reading experience. All the skills and techniques that are required for successful imaginative writing also need to be present in reflective writing.

REFLECTIVE WRITING

The aim here is to give pleasure or interest to the reader. Although information will obviously come into your writing, giving information is not the aim of the exercise. Usually your reflective essay will concern itself with a single idea, insight or experience. It could be sparked by a person, place or object, a relationship, a mood, memory or a photograph, or a feeling, an idea or a belief. Let's look at that in more detail.

WHAT DOES BEING REFLECTIVE MEAN?

Don't be put off by the word 'reflective'. Yes, the essay should be contemplative because you are considering a topic that interests you, but this can be expressed in various ways. The tone might be:

- confidential (taking people into your private thoughts)
- concerned (giving expression to personal worries)
- amused (finding humour in some aspect of your daily life)
- indignant (why is it that some people always assume that ...?).

In fact, a good reflective essay might wander through several of these responses as it contemplates the chosen topic. Make sure that your plan considers all of these potential responses; and make sure, too, that any changes of direction or mood are well signposted.

contd

THE PROCESS OF MAKING UP YOUR MIND

The treatment of your chosen topic should be part of its attraction. It might take the form of someone exploring an idea, examining (and perhaps even discarding) various thoughts before making up their mind:

> Why is it that so many people speak in clichés every time they open their mouths? I'm not an intolerant person but ...
>
> Take my mother, for example: she goes round on a daily round of '............', not to mention, '............' Surely it doesn't take much imagination to ...
>
> I suppose I can understand her position of course. It can't be easy with five youngsters in the house to ransack your mind for original ways to ...
>
> Politicians, too, can't seem to get away from them.
>
> My Polish friend, Monica, sees clichés quite differently from me. She is still learning English and finds that clichés help her ...
>
> But no. On balance, I cannot get away from thinking that people who ...

By the end of your essay, the reader should have a clear sense of your identity and of the things that concern you, amuse you and intrigue you.

USING A FRAMEWORK

You could also take an unobtrusive narrative framework (for example, a visit to an art gallery) as a convenient triggering device through which you reflect on issues and situations. These could take the form of:

- your reflections about, and reactions to, the homeless and their lives from seeing them hanging around the front steps; or

- your reaction to modern art once you were inside; or

- your feelings about being taken around on guided tours.

Be careful, however: a reflective essay of this kind is not a personal essay about a day out you had with the Art Department. In the foreground are the thoughts that were triggered by the event; the factual circumstances of the day should be there only to provide a framework around which to organise your reflections.

 THINGS TO DO AND THINK ABOUT

A reflective essay is a satisfying way to put down on paper some of the recurring ideas that all of us are subject to from time to time: for example, the way some geographical accents get on our nerves, what motivates people to watch cooking programmes and what we feel when meeting new people. With a partner, brainstorm some of the ideas that intrigue, concern, amuse or irritate you. List them and then decide together which of them would give you sufficient depth and variety of angles to sustain reader interest.

 DON'T FORGET

Don't puzzle the reader by jolting suddenly from anxiety one minute to humour the next. Clearly signpost any changes of direction or mood and make a convincing link between them.

 ONLINE TEST

Want to revise your knowledge of this? Head to www.brightredbooks.net and take the test.

 VIDEO LINK

Watch the clip at www.brightredbooks.net for some top tips.

BEING PERSONAL

PERSONAL WRITING

How does a personal essay differ from a reflective one?

Both are embedded in your lived experience, but they are two different ways of regarding similar circumstances. The difference lies perhaps in the **emphasis** which we attribute to these circumstances.

In the previous section, for example, we mentioned how a trip to a gallery with the Art Department could stimulate a variety of reflective angles and provide you with various possibilities for a reflective essay.

The same day out could also give you a good personal essay. Here, the emphasis might be on the preparations, the anticipation, the actual journey, your travelling companions, the programme for the day, memorable parts of the excursion, the feelings you took away from the visit and how your approach to the history of art might have changed.

The reflection that emerges is derived from these events and experiences. This reflection is there to demonstrate that you are capable of viewing biographical material in a way that presents you as a thoughtful person, one who sees significance in what has been experienced and perhaps learned.

BUT NOTHING EVER HAPPENS TO ME!

True, you probably haven't won an Olympic medal or been an *X-Factor* finalist; but successful personal reflective writing doesn't really rely on news-making experiences of this kind. Success in personal reflective writing can stem from very ordinary, everyday experiences or events which, when explored in some detail, reveal that there is a lot more to you and your life than you think. Here are just a few ways of exploring that life.

WHO AM I?

This might seem rather an obvious place to start, but you do need to consider who you think you are as well as who your family, friends and teachers think you are. Are you the person they think you are, or is there another 'you' – one you would like them to see? Or is there another 'you' whom you would rather be? How do you intend to bridge this gap? Talking about incidents or conversations that illustrate these various viewpoints could occupy several sections, with a final section bringing together your verdict on how you view the way forward.

Examining yourself from yet another angle, you might want to write about your present personality compared to the person you used to be when you were younger. How have you changed? What brought about these changes? How do you feel about these changes? You could explore precise events or incidents that might have triggered these changes.

WHAT DO I DO?

Think about what you do when you are not committed to the educational process. Obviously, there are leisure activities and hobbies that help make you the person you are. Consider one activity and how you first became aware of it, your first reactions to it, key incidents along the way, how it has changed you as a person, or what you have gained or learned as a result of the exposure to it.

If you are employed either before or after school or college hours, the possibilities are equally rich in potential. You probably looked for employment because you needed more money, but what did you feel about this? What did you learn as you set about looking for work? How did you react to any upsets along the way? Working with other people poses certain challenges: were there episodes where you learned that the workplace can be very different from school? Using key incidents, illustrate what you have experienced, gained or learned about yourself, people and life generally.

contd

WHAT HAVE I LEARNED?

As we grow and develop, life can deal us all kinds of knocks and bruises. All experience, however, is surely useful for what it teaches us about ourselves and life in general. Failure can sometimes be more instructive than success. Examining disappointment can be a really therapeutic and constructive activity.

On the other hand, sometimes we learn about life through encountering people who have inspired us or taught us without setting out to do so. Watching a friend or family member deal with a difficult situation might teach us about courage, determination or loyalty.

These incidents and these people provide us with material to describe and reflect on in depth.

 ONLINE TEST

How well have you learned this topic? Take the test at www.brightredbooks.net

 ## THINGS TO DO AND THINK ABOUT

With a partner or in a group, look at some of the ways you could examine your own life. Focus on two or three possibilities that you could use as the starting point for a personal essay. Discuss frankly with the group what you might include, and see how others respond to your choices. You might think that the experiences/incidents are interesting, but have they sufficient depth for insightful, thoughtful comment? What did you learn about yourself, other people or life itself?

 ONLINE

For more revision on personal writing, follow the link at www.brightredbooks.net

WRITING DISCURSIVELY

Here you have a choice between writing an argumentative essay, a persuasive essay or a report. We'll deal with the special skills required for report writing later. Let's look first at argumentative and persuasive essays. What exactly are the differences?

- An argumentative essay is one in which you explore and evaluate opposing viewpoints on a controversial topic in formal and strictly neutral language, calling on objective data before offering any final opinion of your own.

- A persuasive essay is one in which you attempt to win over the reader to your view on a controversial topic. Here, too, there will be researched data to substantiate your viewpoint, but it will not be similarly balanced as in an argumentative essay. Contrary viewpoints may be entertained but only to be dismissed. Here the language will be unashamedly emotive with recourse to various rhetorical devices in its attempts to win reader approval.

ARGUMENTATIVE AND PERSUASIVE: THE SHARED ELEMENT

Each option – argumentative or persuasive – offers a radically different approach to a topic. But they also share elements in common. Before you select either one or the other, let's find out what these are.

WHY IS THIS PARTICULAR TOPIC ATTENTION-WORTHY?

No matter which approach you choose, your introduction must establish sufficient background information to convince the reader that the topic is sufficiently important and compelling to be worth reading about – particularly if it is not currently in the news.

IS MY RESEARCH THE BEST AVAILABLE?

In both types of essay, you need to acknowledge your sources at the end. So, how well will your list read?

Nutritional 'facts' from the website of a fast-food manufacturer could hardly be taken to be evidence of sound research.

Website information might be useful as a starting point for topics that have only recently touched our consciousness. So far, these might not have been dealt with in book form, but more traditional topics will have been explored in peer-reviewed publications. The latter are usually the most reliable and authoritative sources.

Quality journals and newspapers employ acknowledged experts and pollsters whose accuracy and readability can usually be counted on. These, of course, can be viewed online, mostly free of charge.

You will impress the marker by providing a balance of paper-based and electronic sources.

Alternatively, try www.idebate.org. Click on the 'Debatabase' strap-line at the top of the Home page, and you will find 14 headings such as Education, Health, Politics, Society, Sport, Science and International, each containing dozens of associated debates with well-articulated arguments for and against. Check out the bibliographic references at the end of each contribution to ensure that there is authoritative backing to the points made.

This Point/Counterpoint format makes it particularly helpful for argumentative essays, although its enormous database of facts makes this site equally useful for persuasive writing, too.

contd

AM I SURE OF THE GENRE FEATURES?

Be careful when you set out to write an argumentative essay that you don't slip into personal views along the way – this will destroy any claim you have to objectivity. Similarly, when you are writing a persuasive essay, be careful not to end up simply presenting information, rather than seeking to persuade.

IS MY INFORMATION UP-TO-DATE?

News is available in multiple media forms 24 hours a day, seven days a week, so there is no excuse for outdated information or statistics. Check the publication dates of books, journals and newspapers and the posting dates of websites before you begin to take notes. This is particularly important in fast-moving research areas such as stem-cell or cloning technology.

HAVE I CHECKED FOR PLAGIARISM?

Be warned! When you are taking notes for your research, do not just 'lift' huge tracts of text and use them without acknowledging them. This is theft, and experienced examiners have a sixth sense for detecting it. Often, this 'lifting' is accidental, but you can avoid any problems by using a highlighter to differentiate quotations from your own notes, and recording the author's name and status, place of publication and date of extract. You could also just put the idea straight into your own words, while acknowledging the author's idea.

SOUNDING AUTHORITATIVE

Whether you are taking the argumentative or persuasive route, you need evidence to back your case, just as you do in your critical essays. In the critical essay, evidence takes the form of close reference to the text or a quotation. In the argumentative or persuasive essay, evidence is the backing of what we call authority. It can take several forms:

- Opinion of an acknowledged expert in the field from, for example, a publication, learned journal, academic website or quality newspaper.
- Poll/survey: findings should be recent. In popular-interest topics, you could consider perhaps a straw poll taken by your year group.
- Official or commissioned reports.

Be careful here, however. Do not overwhelm your case with endless facts; you are being assessed on the quality of the case you are making. Too many facts can obscure this. But without authority of some kind, you are attempting to make a case simply out of your own subjective opinions. You need the added weight that authority can bring. Having some form of expert on both sides of an argumentative essay will help, as will the opinion of a respected source in a persuasive one. But do not overuse authority – it is only there to support **your** case.

THINGS TO DO AND THINK ABOUT

For all their differences, argumentative and persuasive essays share characteristics in common:

- **Illustrative examples or anecdotes** to aid readers' understanding
- **Expert opinion** to support or criticise a point of view
- **Analogies** to suggest parallels with other situations to aid understanding
- **Polls or survey results** to demonstrate research-backed evidence
- **Warnings** to indicate ability to follow through implications of findings.

How they each use these shared features is, of course, very different, as we'll find out later.

ONLINE

If your topic reflects current issues and debates, the chances are that published texts might not have caught up with them fully yet. Online quality journals and newspapers can help greatly here. Key in your topic or issue into the search engine, followed by the quality online newspaper of your choice (for example, the *Independent*, the *Guardian*, the *Herald* or the *Scotsman*) to see what is available.

ONLINE

A useful source of often quite short and readable reports is available at www.brightredbooks.net

DON'T FORGET

You will never be penalised for opinions that run counter to those of the examiner. You are being assessed on the strength of your argued case, not on the nature of your beliefs.

DON'T FORGET

You **must** acknowledge your sources at the end of your essay. A good mix of electronic and published sources looks impressive. Find out how to present them on page 113.

ONLINE TEST

Head to www.brightredbooks.net and take the test on this section.

WRITING ARGUMENTATIVELY

THE ARGUMENTATIVE STRUCTURE: GETTING STARTED

In a successful argumentative essay, the writer takes a topic over which there is some debate and conducts in-depth research before presenting data to support both sides of the argument. They might choose to support one viewpoint or the other. The factual presentation and neutrality of language are the hallmarks of this form of essay.

The opening paragraph is particularly important for establishing your credentials as a reliable investigator of the topic. It needs to suggest that you are:

- reliably informed
- articulate in presenting the opposing viewpoints
- balanced in your assessment of them.

THE PROCESS OF MAKING UP YOUR MIND

So, how might such an opening paragraph look? Let's take a topic and work through its introduction.

The gap year: wasting the present or investing in the future?

After six years of secondary school, most pupils agree that they are ready for a radical change. The question is, of course, what form should that change take? Should they move smartly on to college or university to get started qualifying for the career they have chosen? Or should they postpone tertiary education by taking a gap year before launching into it? And if the choice is to be for a gap year, what form should it take? For some, it is a chance to work to save up for the steadily increasing cost of college life; for others, it is a chance to travel, to volunteer, to teach abroad or simply an opportunity to think about what they want out of life. For its detractors, the gap year is often viewed as a waste of time in years vital for study. For its supporters, it is seen as an investment in life-experience to make that study much more meaningful in the longer term. So, what exactly are the hazards of this year out, and do any advantages gained truly outweigh them?

DON'T FORGET

Always bear in mind that you have a 1300-word limit. Don't get so engrossed in your introduction that you write too much here and have too few words left for arguing both sides of your case.

Balance indicated in title. Note the order in which the alternatives appear.

Significance of topic established in first four sentences.

Topic defined more precisely in sentence five and six.

Sentence seven sets out the opposing argument.

Sentence eight sets out the supporting argument.

Sentence nine suggests how you will approach the development of the essay: negative points first and then the positive ones.

Notice that in the title, in the setting-out of the two arguments and in the final sentence, the positive is mentioned last, hinting perhaps on what side the essay will finally come down.

ORDERING YOUR ARGUMENTS

As in any essay in an exam or portfolio, ideas and arguments should be presented in such a way that the reader is carried effortlessly and smoothly through them. There should be no unexplained, sudden or puzzling changes of direction. Orderly sequencing of arguments is vital in making a convincing case. So, how do you organise a seamless flow of ideas?

One way would be to examine your evidence and then decide where your final verdict falls: are you for or against an idea?

If you were **for** taking a gap year, you might usefully consider the following order of presentation:

- an introduction that sets out both sides, but places the positive second
- subsequent paragraphs/sections that deal with the hazards of taking a gap year
- paragraphs/section that looks at the benefits to be derived from a gap year
- a summative conclusion making clear where you stand on taking a gap year – that is, in favour.

WHY THIS PARTICULAR ORDER?

Suppose you were in favour of taking a gap year but left discussing its hazards until the second half of your essay. Consider, then, the effect on your readers if, in the very next, **concluding** paragraph, you abruptly announced that you were in favour of a process that only a few lines previously you had been expertly criticising. You will puzzle and disconcert them: one minute you are pointing out the shortcomings of an issue, the next you are saying you are in favour of it.

If you are in favour of a topic, discuss its negative points earlier in the essay, so that your positive case seamlessly precedes your positive conclusion. The reader will not have forgotten your negative points, but the positive ones will be fresher in their mind and your approval of them will seem all the more understandable and logical.

The reverse also holds good: if you are **against** an issue, acknowledge its benefits first and then discuss its shortcomings afterwards, so that you lead into a conclusion that follows naturally on from these shortcomings.

If you decide to withhold an opinion of your own because of, for example, current lack of credible evidence, a rapidly changing situation or your own political, social, cultural or educational views, then that's a perfectly legitimate position to take up. Just make sure that you do have good reasons for not committing to an opinion, and that you make these reasons clear – otherwise you risk looking like a ditherer.

 THINGS TO DO AND THINK ABOUT

If you are unsure where you stand on an issue (even after you have conducted considerable research), then try this. Once you have collected your data, organise the points in 'for' and 'against' columns, then try writing an introductory paragraph for **both** sides, in the style of our gap-year introduction. Which version are you more comfortable with? That will hopefully give you the pointer you are looking for.

 ONLINE

If you are looking for somewhere to start, see if any of the argumentative essay topics on this list inspire you: '50 argument essay topics' at www.brightredbooks.net.

 DON'T FORGET

When you are constructing a case in favour of an issue, begin with a point strong enough to gain credibility, develop the case with even stronger points and then finish with your best point. In this way, your argument builds, getting stronger and more impressive as it advances. The opposite sequence creates an unfavourable anti-climax.

 DON'T FORGET

Your flow of ideas will be helped by giving attention to linking words and phrases such as: *Furthermore ... What is more ... On the other hand ....* Remember, too, that picking up a reference from the previous paragraph in the first sentence of the next paragraph can help forward flow. For example: *But it's not enough, however, to examine in isolation the financial advantages of such a move* (the topic of the previous paragraph). *We also need also to take into consideration how a gap year might affect our capacity to study once we return home* (the topic of the upcoming paragraph).

 ONLINE TEST

Head to www.brightredbooks.net and take the test on this section.

WRITING PERSUASIVELY 1

ONLINE

For more inspiration, check out the *Telegraph's* list of the 'Top 25 Political Speeches of All Time' at www.brightredbooks.net

THE LANGUAGE OF PERSUASION

If you have strong opinions on a topic, then this might be a portfolio choice that suits you very well. These opinions need, however, to be credibly supported by researched data, otherwise your essay will sound like an empty rant. There are plenty of models out there for you to study. Try looking in the 'Opinion', 'Comment' or 'Leader' pages of a quality newspaper, or listen to a politician making a speech in parliament. Here are a few techniques to consider:

INVOLVEMENT OF READER

The use of pronouns such as 'we' and 'you' absorb the reader into your arguments, for example:

We are surely alike in thinking that ...

Commands also bring the reader closer:

Consider for a moment ... Think how much better you would feel if ...

EMOTIVE LANGUAGE

You should use emotionally-loaded word choice. This features prominently in much media reporting. 'Families' can become 'hard-working families'; 'Pensioners' can become 'cash-strapped pensioners'; a pregnant woman can become 'a heavily-pregnant woman'. The aim is to arouse sympathy/support for, or anger/criticism against, people and issues in your chosen sphere of persuasive writing. If you cite authority or celebrity figures, then attach emotive phrases to their names: 'Was it not Sir Walter Scott, Scotland's greatest novelist, who claimed that ...?' or 'To quote the much-maligned Tim Henman ...'

RHETORICAL QUESTIONS

These are questions that the reader doesn't expect to answer. They figure prominently in articles, speeches and persuasive essays. They are sometimes answered by the writers themselves to demonstrate their clever mastery of a seemingly difficult problem which they have brought to our attention.

Writers also use them to appeal to our feelings by indirectly suggesting how much we have in common. 'What kind of parent treats children in this way?' 'When will governments learn there is no support for such policies?' Used occasionally – particularly after a passage packed full of emotive word choice – the effect can be powerfully persuasive in stressing shared values. Used too often, they tend to sound rather hollow.

ATTITUDE MARKERS

After some particularly informative yet emotive reporting of information, attitude markers can be useful in guiding reader response:

Clearly, then ... Obviously ... Surely ... Sadly ... Fortunately ...

are just a few. Look out for opportunities to use them to win over readers to your committed stance.

REPETITION

DON'T FORGET

To convince markers that you are serious about being persuasive, make sure your essay uses several persuasive techniques.

Repetition of certain words or phrases is highly emotive. The repetition of parallel structures can also be highly emotive.

In his acceptance speech after the 2012 election, President Obama made full use of them.

'**You'll hear the determination** in the voice of a young field organizer who's working his way through college and wants to make sure every child has that same opportunity. **You'll**

hear the pride in the voice of a volunteer who's going door to door because her brother was finally hired when the local auto plant added another shift. **You'll hear the deep patriotism** in the voice of a military spouse who's working the phones late at night to make sure that no one who fights for this country ever has to fight for a job or a roof over their head when they come home.'

RISING RHETORICAL TRIADS

Don't be put off by their name. You have heard them many times in speeches. They figure prominently in writing that is meant to persuade. They are closely related to the persuasive devices of **repetition** and **parallel structures.** These tripartite statements or phrases typically appear in the final section or paragraph, with each element gaining in strength as the writer seeks to build to a **climax**. 'This is a tramway system which will ... It is a system which will also ... It is a system which, above all, will ...'

Often they combine with rhetorical questions for even greater emotional impact. 'Is this the world we worked for? Is this the world we fought for? And is this a world worth passing on to our children?' Such a ringing closure can work well in a persuasive essay, appealing as it does to the reader's emotional response. It will only work, however, if there is solidly researched data elsewhere in the essay on which you can build such a final emotional pitch.

 THINGS TO DO AND THINK ABOUT

We have already quoted President Obama's acceptance speech after his victory in the 2012 election. He is a master in the use of persuasive techniques. With a partner, list the ones you see here. Pay particular attention to the number of featured phrases that appear in threes. Think about the sense of completeness this gives to the speech. Think about how this could work for you in your essay.

'We believe in a generous America, in a compassionate America, in a tolerant America open to the dreams of an immigrant's daughter who studies in our schools and pledges to our flag, to the young boy on the south side of Chicago who sees a life beyond the nearest street corner, to the furniture worker's child in North Carolina who wants to become a doctor or a scientist, an engineer or an entrepreneur, a diplomat or even a president [...] This country has more wealth than any nation, but that's not what makes us rich. We have the most powerful military in history, but that's not what makes us strong. Our university, our culture are all the envy of the world, but that's not what keeps the world coming to our shores. What makes America exceptional are the bonds that hold together the most diverse nation on Earth, the belief that our destiny is shared, that this country only works when we accept certain obligations to one another and to future generations [...] That's what makes America great.'

 DON'T FORGET

The novelist Joseph Conrad once remarked:

He who wants to persuade should put his trust not in the right argument, but in the right word. The power of sound has always been greater than the power of sense.

With a partner or in a group, discuss whether you agree with Conrad. Do you see any dangers in this belief for you as a persuasive essay writer?

 ONLINE TEST

Want to revise your knowledge of this? Head to www.brightredbooks.net and take the test.

WRITING PERSUASIVELY 2

FIRST THOUGHTS

In the persuasive essay, unlike the argumentative essay, you are unashamedly out to persuade readers to adopt your point of view. But enthusiasm and persuasive techniques are not enough: you need to present yourself as an authoritative advocate for your topic. So, how do you do that?

ORDERING YOUR ARGUMENTS

If you want to persuade readers of the rightness of your case, you need to marshal your arguments just as carefully as you would in an argumentative essay. To win over readers, it's wise to establish yourself as a sensible, reasonable person. And sensible, reasonable people are always aware that their opinion is not the only one around.

How, then, do you deal with possibly contrary viewpoints when you are out to make out your own persuasive case?

As in an argumentative essay, it might be wise to deal with them early on in your essay so that your increasingly powerful arguments push them aside in the memory of your readers.

This might be a possible solution:

- An introduction in which you make your viewpoint abundantly clear.
- Acknowledge perhaps a conflicting opinion but refute it in a reasonable, logical way. It is always a good idea to show respect to contrary views. But do this briefly!
- Launch your first persuasive paragraph.
- Continue with similarly persuasive paragraphs, saving your strongest argument until last.
- Conclusion.

WHAT MAKES A PERSUASIVE OPENING?

Now that we've looked at some of the overall structuring features of the essay, let's look at how the introduction to that essay might look in practice.

Here is someone keen to make the case for reducing university courses to two years in length.

You and your degree: how to cut costs and maintain quality

It's difficult to say what worries some school leavers most: not getting into university or not being able to afford it once there. Stories of debt totalling £20,000 or £30,000 after a three-year course are not uncommon. So, what would you say to an idea that could cut the cost dramatically yet maintain the standard expected by demanding employers? Well, by teaching students for 40 weeks a year rather than less than 30 (which seems to be about the norm at the moment), a similar amount of teaching could be achieved, to allow students to arrive at degree standard much quicker. That's how the University of Buckingham has cut degree time from three to two years – and, judging by their high ranking in the comparative league tables, there is no falling-off in academic standards. Surely, this is an approach that needs looking into, not just for cash-strapped students like us but for staff and the rest of the struggling university sector, also?

contd

Note title is itself committed to persuasion, using both 'you' and your' and parallel structures: 'cut cost'/'maintain standards'.

Concerns defined and explained in first two sentences.

Third sentence offers an attractive possible solution in the form of a rhetorical question.

Solution explained and its significance established in sentences four and five.

Sentence six begins with a persuasive attitude marker and hints at running order of the essay itself, with recourse to some emotive language: 'cash-strapped students'/'struggling university sector'

Read this introduction in conjunction with our list of persuasive features, and you will see that this essay is well-launched on its persuasive path. You might try counting the number of techniques used in one fairly brief paragraph. Keep this approach in mind when you launch your own persuasive introduction. Keep checking that you are being persuasive and not just informative.

KEEPING UP THE PERSUASION

As we said, there is a danger in persuasive writing of lapsing into the merely informative. The other danger of persuasive writing is that it is possible to end up having a good old rant, rather than presenting a genuinely persuasive essay. Enthusiasm and persuasive techniques need to be balanced by authoritative delivery. So, how might you achieve this?

One way might be to ensure that your evidence matches up to your claims and that your evidence is persuasively 'sold' to the reader. In other words, use the SEC structure from the critical essay and overlay it with persuasive language and techniques.

Here's how a body paragraph might look in our essay:

Statement	A still further advantage of shorter courses is that mature students, often a sadly neglected sector of the student body, can participate much more freely in university work. Imagine the personal and crippling financial cost of taking three whole years out of family life! Imagine how much more enthusiastic you would be about if you knew you could cut that by a third!
Evidence	Commenting recently to BBC News on the promising uptake of mature students in these shorter courses, Director for Academic Development at Stafford University, Dr Steve Wyn Williams, pointed out: 'Mature students want focused, cost-effective courses that do not require them to take three or more years out of a career. Many of our students who opt to do the fast-tracks are mature students who are looking for career change. They are often quite used to working during the summer period when they were in employment.'
Commentary	So, not only do students benefit greatly by saving time and money, the nation's economy benefits enormously, too. Mature students who previously would never have ventured into a lengthy three-year stint in academia are clearly seeing the advantages of these time-conscious courses. In so doing, they are not only empowering themselves but also enriching the country with additional skills and vital expertise to allow Britain to compete in the growing global economy. Who could quibble with that?

 ## THINGS TO DO AND THINK ABOUT

The information on two-year university courses came from www.idebate.org. Key 'two-year courses' into the 'Search by keyword box'. Use the information that you find there to help you write the introduction to a persuasive essay disagreeing with the idea of two-year courses.

DON'T FORGET

Persuasive techniques are not just for the introduction. You need to keep them up throughout the entire essay. Beware of slipping into the merely informative.

 ONLINE TEST

How well have you learned this topic? Take the test at www.brightredbooks.net

REPORT WRITING

In the world of work, reports are written for busy people who need key information to be presented clearly and concisely. This requires clarity of expression and a logically-ordered structure that often employ numbered and/or titled sub-headings. Given the 1300-word limit, you need to apportion space carefully.

PLANNING YOUR REPORT

Many of the preliminary steps in preparing a successful report are the same as those required for argumentative essay writing.

RESEARCH TECHNIQUES	PLANNING PROCEDURES
• When searching through either paper-based or electronic media sources for authority, you must be careful to discriminate between objective fact and subjective opinion. • Opinion, of course, is perfectly valid if you are recording the views of polls or surveys you have conducted for this exercise, for it is these views that will give you 'authority' for your material in later recommendations that you might make. • Check sources for independence of viewpoint. '.org' or '.ac' often carries more authority than '.com'. • Be alert to the risk of plagiarism. Use your source material in your own words. • Note down exact sources as you work. It will save you time when you come to prepare a bibliography at the end.	• Researching and planning a successful report will probably take far more time than actually writing it. Make sure that the research is the most thorough possible. Time spent here will pay dividends later. • Group your research findings in the way that you do for a critical essay. The mind-map or list will serve equally well; this will help determine how many areas each section will require. • Determine the running order, remembering that a good report – like a good essay – requires an introduction and a conclusion. • Keep language neutral and formal: no abbreviations, colloquialisms or figurative language. Nevertheless, language should be crisp and sentences well-formed to make complex ideas clear. Pay as much attention to linking sentences smoothly as you would in any essay.

THE FOUR-PART FORMULA

Reports can be structured in a variety of ways, but you will find that this four-part formula can often be useful:

Introduction	The neutral language will be very similar to that employed in an argumentative essay. The significance of topic will be explored, the purpose of the report made clear and the sources acknowledged. Here's an example: *1. Introduction* *In our swiftly-changing society, the high street has become …* *The purpose of this report is to give an overview of how various sectors of the community view …* *In preparing this report, we have consulted …*
Findings	In neutral language, you will interpret what your research has discovered, subdivided as appropriate: *2. Findings* *There was general concern among the public at large that the high street was rapidly becoming …* *2.1 Shopkeepers felt let down by the council's failure to support local traders in …* *2.2 Shoppers felt that the high-street experience was now beginning to feel as if …* *2.3 60 per cent of young people interviewed said they now felt that …*
Discussion	Here you begin to interpret findings for the reader: *3. Discussion* *It can be seen that shopkeepers and shoppers were united in believing that much more could be achieved if …* *The concerns of young people were noticeably different, however, in that their chief worry involved late-night security around …*
Conclusion	Depending on the type of report you are writing, you could have various conclusions: signalling benefits to be derived from a certain course of action; suggesting solutions to ongoing problems or giving warnings about failure to intervene: *4. Conclusion* *While there was no unanimity as to future action required to safeguard the future of the high street, there was some consensus over … With only marginally increased costs, it might be possible to reinvigorate town-centre life by … and …* *Failure to do so may well lead to a situation in which …*

ADDING PROFESSIONALISM

Some of your report's information and findings can be conveyed by diagrams, pie charts, graphs, tables or bullet points. Make sure that graphic items are adequately captioned. But make sure also that you actually discuss them in your text, otherwise their inclusion might simply puzzle the marker.

Consider, too, how your presentation could be enhanced by adding a separate title page in which you give the report's title, the date of presentation and your name. A separate sheet at the end with a precisely documented list of sources will add to the professional air of the document.

CITING SOURCES IN DISCURSIVE WRITING

Earlier in this section, we mentioned the importance of providing sources for discursive writing. Naturally, the more professionally you present the resources you have consulted, the more seriously your work will be taken. It will also be useful when you go on to college or university to know how to set out your sources correctly. There are several recognised ways of setting out sources. The following one is known as APA style (American Psychological Association) and is commonly used in British academic institutions.

REFERENCING BOOKS

To reference books in the APA style:

Start with author's name: surname first, then initial. (Followed by the year of publication in brackets) *then comes the title in italics.* Then the city of publication: and finally the publisher.

A complete book reference should appear like this:

King, R. (2000) *Brunelleschi's Dome.* London: Penguin.

REFERENCING NEWSPAPERS AND MAGAZINE ARTICLES

To reference articles from newspapers or magazines:

Start with author's name: surname first, then initial. (Followed by the publication date in brackets) Next include the title of the article itself. *Then the name of the publication should come in italics.* And finally the page reference.

A complete article reference should appear like this:

Goring, R. (4 January 2003) She's Talking Our Language Now. *The Herald.* p14.

REFERENCING ELECTRONICALLY SOURCED MATERIAL

To reference electronically sourced material:

Give the name of author (if available) and title of article/publication as you would for a print publication. In place of city of publication and name of publisher, put the web address and the date when the article was posted (if available) and also the date when you accessed it.

THINGS TO DO AND THINK ABOUT

Practise your bibliography skills by setting out the texts below in correct APA style.

Recently I came across a helpful book called A Good Night Out. It was published by Eyre Methuen and was written by John McGrath. It was published in 1981. The publisher is located in London.

An interesting novel, published in 2014, is Gone are the Leaves. It was published in Edinburgh by Canongate and the writer is the Glasgow-based author Anne Donovan.

Students of the unusual may be interested in an article in the *Guardian* written by Kim Willsher. The article is called Oh l'amour: Paris rail bridge collapses under weight of too much love. It appeared on page 24 of the edition of the 9th June 2014.

DON'T FORGET

In topics of current/topical interest, your 'authority' could derive from a straw poll taken in your year group, town centre or some similar place where you are likely to get a good cross-section of opinion. If you can cross-refer this to, say, a newspaper or magazine article, you could end up with an impressive report, blending published data with your own findings. Ensure that your poll questions are sharply focused on the information you require.

DON'T FORGET

A report will often require you to convey and interpret complex information from published and electronic sources. Make sure you do not lapse into plagiarism. Your paraphrasing skills are vitally important in report writing.

ONLINE

For the kind of language and structure used in reports by real-world bodies, try looking at the Scottish Government link at www.brightredbooks.net. Some of the shorter ones might well give you ideas for your own research.

ONLINE

For more information on listing web addresses, consult the link at www.brightredbooks.net. See point 6.9 under Web Pages.

ONLINE TEST

Head to www.brightredbooks.net and take the test on this section.

LISTENING AND TALKING – WHAT SKILLS ARE SHARED?

So far, we've covered critical reading and critical writing skills in this Guide. Now it's time to look at skills for listening and talking (in group and solo mode).

ONLINE

Check out the article about how important listening skills are in business at www.brightredbooks.net

THE IMPORTANCE OF LISTENING AND DISCUSSING

You not only need these skills for your course – they are also two of the most important skills you can acquire for your career beyond school.

Whether you want to work in the world of commerce, public service, academia, science, medicine or media, you'll discover that you have to spend a great deal of your time attending meetings of one kind or another. Being able to function effectively in this environment will be a great career plus.

Let's look first at effective listening and how to acquire effective listening techniques.

BEING AN EFFECTIVE LISTENER

If we're honest with ourselves, we all have a tendency to be lazy listeners. We switch on the TV, we select an MP3 track, we ask a friend how they are – and then we get distracted. The sounds carry on, but our mind is often elsewhere, although, if challenged, we will hotly claim that we have been 'listening'. Effective listening requires mental discipline. So, how do we acquire the discipline of focusing accurately on the aims and purposes of what is being said and filter out the distractions around us? Here's a simple checklist for good listening behaviour:

CHECK OUT AIMS AND PURPOSES

What are the speaker's aims? Do they want to convey information, persuade you to adopt a certain viewpoint, analyse a critical situation or simply entertain? Perhaps the speaker will have more than one aim and will entertain us to persuade us to share a viewpoint. Be alert to such possible cross-overs, and constantly monitor content to ascertain central aims. Check, too, whether the ideas are being backed by convincing information/statistics or are merely claims or opinions.

ADOPT A POSITIVE ATTITUDE TO THE SUBJECT

Perhaps on the surface the subject does not appear particularly interesting to you. You cannot, however, afford to lose concentration. The greatest mark-loser is to listen passively, letting the information wash over you. Listen actively, do not make negative assumptions about the interest or complexity of what you are going to hear, and keep alert. You might be surprised by the turn the talk takes.

ADOPT A POSITIVE ATTITUDE TO THE SPEAKER

Ignore distractions such as appearance, personality, weak delivery, accent or mannerisms. It's the message, not the messenger, that counts. And do not lose concentration or patience because they adopt an opinion that does not coincide with yours.

contd

AVOID EXTERNAL DISTRACTIONS

The view from the window, whispering behind you, the heat in the room, pre-lunch rumbling from your stomach: they are all very human distractions which can disturb concentration long enough to miss a key point.

CONCENTRATE ON CENTRAL IDEAS

Don't let interesting stories or examples blind you to the reason for their inclusion in the talk. They are there to illustrate a point; they are not usually the point in themselves. Are there clues in the opening statements that indicate what the central ideas of the upcoming sections might be? Note them down. Listen for ideas, not individual words.

BE ALERT TO THE NON-VERBAL

Emotions are less easy to control than words. Skilled listening means listening for messages that the speaker's voice, rather than their words, might be signalling unconsciously. As in group discussion, body language can also give hints to the real message.

MAKE NOTES THAT MATTER

Trying to jot down everything that's said is not only impossible, it's distracting you from what **is** being said. Make notes brief, concentrating on key ideas and key words or phrases. And write them so they are readable afterwards!

KEY INTENTION INDICATORS

Making sense of spoken communication requires you to be alert on several fronts. As well as being tuned in to the factual information being presented, you also need to listen for signals that tell you the intended **purpose** of the communication and the **audience** at whom it is aimed. If you are aware of these considerations, you will be better equipped to understand and assess the speaker's success or failure in communicating with you.

A speaker can have a number of different aims, whether they are participating in a group discussion, a lecture or a talk. Let's take a look at some of these aims and at the language that is used to achieve them.

PURPOSE	SOME POSSIBLE MARKERS
Inform/Raise awareness	• Neutral, unemotional language • Balanced arguments and structure • Factual reporting
Analyse	• Subject-specific vocabulary • Technical statistics and data • Complex sentences
Persuade/Reassure/Inspire	• Emotive vocabulary • Rhetorical questions • Repetition • Targeted climaxes
Entertain	• Colloquial vocabulary • Chatty expressions, short sentences • Anecdotes • Exaggeration

 ONLINE TEST

How well have you learned this topic? Take the test at www.brightredbooks.net

 ONLINE

Check out this clip about active listening: 'How to be a good listener: Good listeners; Active listening' at www.brightredbooks.net

 DON'T FORGET

In the course of the address, the speaker could have more than one aim. If, for example, the intention is **to persuade** or **to inform** us, they might want **to entertain** us occasionally to make the point all the more effective. Be alert to shifts of approach and what lies behind them.

 THINGS TO DO AND THINK ABOUT

To try out your listening skills, key in 'Elizabeth Gilbert: Success, failure and the drive to keep creating' (www.ted.com) into your browser. Listen to the talk. Then, with the aid of the grid above, think about what the speaker's purpose was. Or did she have several purposes? What markers helped you determine your answers? Discuss this with a partner before tackling the following questions.

FOCUSED LISTENING PRACTICE

HOW GOOD A LISTENER AM I?

Before you practise the type of listening exercise that you will have in your Unit assessment, have a look at how you can boost your general listening skills.

Often, when we are engaged in a listening exercise, distractions occur, concentration flags and part of the passage passes without us really absorbing what has been said. In an assessment, the part you miss could be the section that some of the questions are on. We'll look at how to guard against this happening.

SPOT THE CHANGES

With a partner, choose a passage of roughly 20/30 lines from a book; a passage from that part of a set text you have not yet read would be fine. You are going to read out two versions of this passage to the class: your version will be exactly as it is printed in the book; your partner will read out the same passage but with subtle changes that you have agreed together. Change perhaps a short phrase, a name, an adverb, a verb, a time of day or a place name. Agree as a class how many changes you are looking for.

Once both versions have been read out, check out which member of the class has recorded the highest number of noted changes. It might surprise you how many changes slip by without being noticed!

HOW WELL WERE YOU LISTENING?

Here is another way to tone up your listening skills. Appoint a quizmaster (male or female) from the class. Select a group of people who will answer the questions. Agree as a class the number and type of questions the quizmaster will ask the group – for example, 'What do you do in your spare time?' 'Do you have a part-time job?' 'What is it?' 'Do you support a football team?' 'If so, what team is it?' 'What do you hope to do after leaving school?'

The others note down their answers. The quizmaster will also have been listening to the responses (perhaps with the help of a scribe) and then will ask a series of random questions selected from the answers he/she has heard, for example, 'Which three members of the class support Arsenal?' 'Who works part-time in a Chinese restaurant?' 'How many people hope to study in Glasgow?' It will emerge fairly quickly how well – or otherwise – you have been listening.

PRACTISING FOR THE ASSESSMENT

Listen again to the Elizabeth Gilbert talk we heard in the 'Things to Do and Think About' section on the previous page. Here, Gilbert, author of best-selling *Eat, Pray, Love*, discusses her approach to success and failure in life ('Elizabeth Gilbert: Success, failure and the drive to keep creating' (www.ted.com)). Now play it again in sections. Take notes as you listen, then answer the following questions. Use your own words as far as possible.

contd

SECTION FROM BEGINNING TO 2 MINUTES 06 SECONDS

1   Identify one purpose of the talk. Explain your answer with evidence.

2   Identify two possible audiences for the talk. Give evidence for your choices.

3   Explain how effective you find this section as an introduction to the talk, referring to the speaker's use of language.

SECTION FROM 2 MINUTES 06 SECONDS TO 3 MINUTES 14 SECONDS

4   The speaker has a slightly unusual interpretation of what 'going home' means to her. Explain in your own words what this expression means to her.

5   Gilbert's love of writing, she tells us, is intensely felt. In your own words, explain three ways that the power of this love is displayed.

SECTION FROM 3 MINUTES 14 SECONDS TO 4 MINUTES 41 SECONDS

6   Talking of the unsuccessful young waitress she had been, and the successful author she had become with *Eat Pray, Love*, Gilbert asks: 'Why did I suddenly feel I was like her [the waitress] all over again?'

   In your own words, explain what, in Gilbert's mind, the failure of the waitress and the success of the author had in common.

SECTION FROM 4 MINUTES 41 SECONDS TO END

7   Identify **two** rhetorical devices in this section and explain their effects. (To remind yourself what rhetorical devices are, look at the techniques for writing a persuasive essay on page 108.)

8   Gilbert makes a link between herself and her audience as she winds up her talk.

   a   Explain the link.

   b   Explain the effectiveness of trying to make this link at this point in her talk.

THINGS TO DO AND THINK ABOUT

To get into the spirit of listening actively, watch or listen carefully to an evening news bulletin. At the end, ask yourself how many stories were dealt with in the headlines, how many of these news items referred to Britain, how many to Europe and how many to the rest of the world. How many would be of particular interest to teenagers? Think about your reasons for saying this, and be prepared to justify your response. It's all good practice for success in a listening-outcome assessment.

DON'T FORGET

Remember that the purpose of a written text can have much in common with a spoken one like Elizabeth Gilbert's. Make sure that you are aware of the most common purposes and how they are marked in speeches and written texts. Check both out on page 115.

DON'T FORGET

When you are asked about possible audiences for a certain spoken or written text, you need to think not only about content and the type of people the topic might appeal to (and here common sense is the surest guide), but also about the tone. For example, is it chatty/colloquial and full of anecdotes? Factual? Emotive? The tone will tell you a lot about the degree of commitment of the speakers. And that, in turn, might help you identify who they are: for example, are they people with a passing interest in x, people with a previous knowledge of x or people who are seriously committed to x? Whoever you identify, make sure that you have specific items of textual evidence to back up your claim.

DON'T FORGET

If you are asked to comment on rhetorical devices, remember that these are the devices you include in a good persuasive essay. (Go to page 108 if you need to jog your memory.)

ONLINE TEST

Head to www.brightredbooks.net and take the test on this section.

TALKING EFFECTIVELY IN DISCUSSION

HOW DO WE MEASURE SUCCESS IN DISCUSSION?

In a group discussion, a number of participants exchange information and opinions on a given topic, problem or issue. Although they might or might not achieve agreement, each participant has an obligation to make a significant contribution to the discussion if it is to succeed. In a discussion, listening is not enough; everyone needs to participate.

As a participant in a discussion, you must approach the group with an open mind, genuinely prepared to listen as well as to argue your point of view. It is an activity in which you can use your knowledge of the techniques of **persuasion** to help you succeed. As you speak, think about how you might introduce, say, **repetition** or **attitude markers** or **rhetorical questions**. Think, too, about the other techniques you could employ. Check out the list of persuasive techniques on pages 108–111. They could add to your authority and boost your self-confidence.

In a good group discussion, you will probably hear views with which you strongly disagree, but you must respect your opponent's point of view and his or her right to hold it if you want your own opinions to be accorded the same courtesy.

WHAT ARE THE ORAL SKILLS REQUIRED?

You now know quite a lot about listening skills. But what about the oral skills you will need when you are participating in a discussion? Here are some tips:

BE CONCISE

Other people are waiting to take part; make your case fully but avoid being too long-winded. Don't hog the discussion!

BE CLEAR

Clear expression is a sign of clear thinking. Avoid complicated sentences that will lose the attention of your fellow participants. Present ideas in a logical order that is easy to follow.

BE NATURAL

Remember that you are talking to people, not at them. Anything which sounds rehearsed sounds stilted, false and generally unconvincing. Cultivate a natural-sounding delivery in straightforward language. If you have an accent, be proud of it. It is part of you.

BE POSITIVE

Present persuasively the benefits/advantages of your viewpoint rather than insist on the shortcomings/disadvantages of your opponent's. When you need to disagree, do so politely in unaggressive language.

BE PERSUASIVE

Be careful not to sound threatening in your approach to the topic. Use language with which others can agree. Remember, you are seeking support for your views. Win them over with your reasonable-sounding, considered stance. Use some of the persuasive techniques you learnt about when writing persuasive essays on pages 108–111.

BE REACTIVE

Don't be shy about picking up a point made by someone else and asking them to explain it further. Seeking clarification is an excellent way of moving on a discussion. React, too, to the level of formality of the discussion. Sometimes, practice discussions might be fairly informal affairs; at other times, you will need to adopt a more formal tone for more serious assessment discussions.

DON'T FORGET

A successful group discussion should leave all participants feeling they have contributed meaningfully to a full and balanced exploration of a subject. If you feel unhappy with your contribution, what will you do next time to improve matters?

DON'T FORGET

A good discussion will often find you getting emotionally involved. But don't lose your temper over views with which you disagree or with the people putting them forward. Keep your language calm if you wish first to win and then retain the support of neutral members of the group. Nobody likes Mr or Miss Angry!

ONLINE TEST

Want to revise your knowledge of this? Head to www.brightredbooks.net and take the test.

ONLINE

For some tips at how to contribute well in group discussions, head to www.brightredbooks.net

THINGS TO DO AND THINK ABOUT

Think about and discuss with a partner how successful or otherwise you find the following extracts from a group discussion:

- How appropriate and/or persuasive would you rate these comments to be?

- Where do you feel the participants have gone wrong, and what alternative ways of expression would you suggest?

Use the above guidelines to help you evaluate. Identify any persuasive techniques you note being used.

> That's a very interesting point. But surely you're not saying that the High Street has no future?

> Yes, he's made mistakes. Yes, he's upset people. But what kind of human being never puts a foot wrong?

> For goodness sake, man, will you stop going on about wages! You seem to think it's all about money. Tell him, Sheila!

> You have no evidence for any of this. You come in here with a half-baked case for cloning, but you have not produced a single piece of hard evidence. Do you think we haven't noticed?

> I see where you're coming from, but, well ..., when you think about it, is it ..., I mean, ... where does this get us? Are we, well ... better off or worse off? I dunno.

> Briony's point is a sound one. She's made a really clear case for taking action right away. Who's with me in supporting her in the next move? Neil?

A DISCUSSION IS MORE THAN ORAL SKILLS

DON'T FORGET

Be an active listener as well as an active talker. Follow what others are saying. Show by your facial expression that you are taking in what is being said, whether as a supporter or critic. It helps speakers to gauge how well or badly they are getting through to their listeners.

DON'T FORGET

Note-taking while others are speaking suggests serious engagement with what is being said. You'll also find taking notes helpful if you want to seek clarification, if you support or disagree with particular points or if you want to use the information in an essay of your own later on.

IS MY BODY LANGUAGE HELPING MY CASE?

A successful group discussion is not just about **what** you say; it is also about **how** you say it. You need to show yourself as being part of a group as well as part of a discussion. That means being as aware of your body language as of your oral input. For instance, what signals does slouching back in your chair send out? Or stabbing your finger in the air to make a point?

One researcher has suggested that between 60 and 70 per cent of all meaning is derived from non-verbal behaviour. Clearly, how you sit and behave in the course of the discussion matters, so we'll take a look at what body language adds to group discussions.

BODY POSTURE

Find a comfortable position to sit in that suggests interest and alert-but-relaxed engagement in the discussion. Slumping back in your chair might suggest boredom; leaning too far forward might suggest aggression.

EYE CONTACT

Engage with the group as a whole. Fixing your attention on any one member might suggest lack of confidence; looking around the group reassures members that you are addressing them all and that you value everyone's opinion.

HAND GESTURES

Many people find it natural to express themselves with hand movements as well as words. This is not a problem unless the gestures hint at aggression – for example, finger-pointing or table-thumping – or if they become distracting and irritating to the group.

FINDING A ROLE

You now know how to listen, and you now know how to react orally and physically in a discussion. Is there anything else you can do to get the most out of a discussion?

You could allocate roles to the various group members, so that once you know your role, you could intervene appropriately and get the discussion moving forward positively.

contd

THE CHAIRPERSON

The chairperson or leader will:

- introduce the topic and suggest what form the discussion will take
- invite each member of the group to participate in turn
- ensure the group remains on task/topic
- ensure a balanced discussion, encouraging quieter members to talk and discouraging any one member from dominating the discussion
- intervene when there is a threat of conflict between members.

THE REPORTER

The reporter or recorder will:

- make notes of the key points made during the discussion
- summarise the outcome, outlining any divisions of opinion that emerged
- report back to the class on the findings of the group.

THE INDIVIDUAL MEMBER

Each individual group member will:

- provide personal, relevant and substantial ideas/opinions/experiences
- take account of what others have to say, show support, raise questions or doubts and seek clarification when necessary
- make notes on points that might be raised later as a result of the contribution of others
- avoid interrupting the contributions of others until they are complete.

MAXIMISING OUTCOMES

A good group discussion will often arouse strong feelings in the participants. Open conflict, however, is the enemy of progress in a discussion. Good group-discussion manners require us all to choose our language carefully and think of the feelings of others when we formulate our comments. That doesn't mean you avoid making your point strongly; you just do it in a way that doesn't upset the atmosphere in the group. This means the debate doesn't hit a brick wall of hostility.

Everything we've said here is about creating an atmosphere in which profitable discussion can flourish. If everyone is included and respected and everyone's opinion is valued, then discussion progresses, knowledge is enriched and understanding increases. A good discussion, a commentator once remarked, should generate more light than heat. Be careful to ensure that your discussions do just that: create helpful enlightenment, not pointless hot air.

 THINGS TO DO AND THINK ABOUT

There is nothing like a group discussion for defining personality. What kind of personality do **you** project in a group discussion? To see if you recognise yourself, tap '6 types of student you will meet in a group discussion' into YouTube for a very brief overview of personality types. You might feel this is an oversimplification of behaviour, but it is thought-provoking. To what extent do you agree with what is being said about the personalities of group participants?

 DON'T FORGET

Over the course of the term, it is a good idea to rotate the roles of chairperson and reporter around all members of the group so that everyone gets the benefit of developing these important life-skills.

 DON'T FORGET

Criticise an idea by all means, but don't attack the person putting it forward. Use reason, not emotion, to show up what you think the shortcomings of the idea or argument are.

 ONLINE

Much of what we have been saying here applies to the academic world in which you currently find yourselves. For the perspective of group discussion in the world of work, try following the link at www.brightredbooks.net. Scroll down to the bottom of the page, and you will find no fewer than seventeen different sections on this topic!

ONLINE TEST

Head to www.brightredbooks.net and take the test on this section.

TALKING EFFECTIVELY: GOING SOLO

The skills we have been focusing on in this unit will make you a much more effective listener and a considerably more persuasive participant in a group discussion. And they will also develop your ability to give a solo talk, because by listening to expert talkers such as Elizabeth Gilbert you have been exposed to some of the techniques for engaging an audience with your topic. And by intervening in group discussions you are learning how best to put across your point of view to win approval. A solo persuasive talk is merely an extension of these skills. Like a group discussion, it is a useful way to deal with a unit assessment.

GETTING ORGANISED: MAKING USE OF YOUR RESEARCH

If you have already written a persuasive essay for either the portfolio or a written unit assessment, you could recycle the research you have done for this and use it as the basis for a persuasive talk. Here's how you could do this:

LISTEN TO THE BEST

Once you hear how experienced talkers go about holding an audience's attention, you will be more able to adapt their persuasive techniques to your own subject. Here are just a few expert talkers available at the www.ted.com website.

Sarah Lewis: *Embrace the near win*
Notice her use of an initial anecdote, followed by a question which she proceeds to answer in a variety of ways: this gives the talk its shape.

Notice her use of repetition: 'Mastery is not ...'

What other tips can you collect here about delivery of a solo talk?

Del Harvey: *The strangeness of scale at Twitter*
Here we have several rhetorical questions that lead into real questions: 'What do I mean by "visualize catastrophe"?' ... 'I try to think of how something ...'

Notice how she gets close to her audience with her use of 'let's ...', 'you' and 'we'.

What other means does she employ to win over her audience?

Tony Shapshak: *You don't need an app for* that
Here the speaker makes an ingenious case for persuading the audience that Africa is a centre of innovation.

Notice how he uses rhetorical questions and humour to great effect. What else can we learn here?

While you are listening, note down the persuasive techniques that you hear at work. Good listening is the basis of good talking.

REVISIT PERSUASIVE TECHNIQUES

On page 108, we looked at some of the basic techniques for persuading readers to adopt your point of views in a written text. These techniques will work equally well in a solo talk context. Indeed, some of the examples detailed there originated in successful speeches.

DECIDE ON A STRUCTURE

A good persuasive talk requires as much, attention to structure as a good essay if not more, because listeners don't have a text to refer to, and they need reassurance that it's going to be easy for them to follow what you're saying. That reassurance comes in the

ONLINE

You can find links to each of these talks at www.brightredbooks.net

contd

form of early signposting. This could take many forms: for example, you could begin with a question, and use the answers to this question to form the basis of the rest of the talk; or you could itemise the areas to be covered at the beginning of the talk and then working through them, one by one; or you could contrast a past situation with the present. The nature of your subject will probably dictate the talk's structure – but always make sure there is one, and indicate it early on.

REMEMBER A TALK IS NOT AN ESSAY

Although a persuasive essay and a persuasive talk have much in common, they are not the same thing. An essay is meant to be read; a talk is meant to be listened to. Listeners do not have a text in front of them, so they can't go back to read something they have not quite understood. A talk must therefore be easy to follow. That means sentence structure must be considered even more fully than in an essay. Keep sentences fairly short (this makes life easier for the listener), and keep them easy to articulate (this makes life easier for you). Stumbling over long-winded sentences is a sure-fire way to lose your audience.

Repetition and parallel structures are particularly useful in talks, since the listeners are being prepared for what is to come. For proof of this, look at the extracts from the Barack Obama speech in the 'Repetition' section of persuasive techniques on pages 108–109.

CONTROL BODY LANGUAGE

The best talk in the world can be undermined by body language that irritates or distracts. Go back and check what we said on page 120 about body language in group discussions. Much of that advice is equally valid in a solo talk.

MONITOR VOICE PRODUCTION

You don't need to sound like Liam Neeson to succeed in a solo talk. But you **do** need to be able to vary your tone regularly to avoid droning on in a monotone – a certain way to lose your audience, no matter how gripping the topic. Think, too, about slowing down from time to time to emphasise certain points, then pick up speed again. Vary the pace as you would vary sentence structure in an essay – it keeps your audience engaged with you.

KEEP TO YOUR PURPOSE

In a persuasive talk, never lose sight of this purpose. By all means inform and entertain, but keep focused on your key intention as you present your material. Make sure you have built in a variety of the persuasive techniques. Don't overuse any particular one.

PRACTISE AT HOME

The bathroom mirror is a great audience! As is the family dog! Don't give the first run-through of your talk at the assessment. Try it out several times on anyone who will listen. Get the feel of it in your mouth. Change any words you stumble over, and shorten any sentences that are difficult to say.

ONLINE TEST

How well have you learned this topic? Take the test at www.brightredbooks.net

VIDEO LINK

For more good examples of speeches, watch the clips at www.brightredbooks.net

THINGS TO DO AND THINK ABOUT

If you have already written a persuasive essay, go back and examine what you would need to do to turn it into a persuasive talk. How will your opening need to change? How will sentence structure need to be revised for the listener? Will any quotations need shortening or paraphrasing? Which persuasive techniques would improve your talk? Which personal pronouns will you be using?

If you haven't already written a persuasive essay, try sketching out a persuasive talk on the following topic:

> **Speaking a foreign language increases the quality of life.**

This is a topic which does not really require intensive research but can be put together quite quickly. See how you get on making persuasive techniques work for you.

ANSWERS

Here some possible answers to the questions that you have tackled. There will often be variations on these that are also acceptable. If in doubt, consult your teacher.

UNDERSTANDING QUESTIONS, PAGE 11

1 **Extract from Charles Montgomery, 'The secrets of the world's happiest cities', in the *Guardian*, 1 November 2013**

   a The city experience (1) is just as much about travelling through it (1) as simply finding yourself there. (1)

   b The writer implies that cycle rides are best enjoyed when the temperature is warm (1). He tells that 'Judge's confession would have been unremarkable' (1) if the January temperature where he lived had not usually averaged −17°C, suggesting his shock at cycling in such temperatures. (1)

   c The city noises became hushed. (1)

   Twilight brought about beautiful colours in the sky. (1)

   The snow would act as a mirror to these colours. (1)

   He enjoyed hearing his son behind him breathing in the cold air. (1)

   He felt he and his son had both become part of the season itself. (1)

2 **Extract from Peter Oborne, 'Yes, the floods are awful, but we must keep a sense of proportion', in the *Daily Telegraph*, 12 February 2014**

   a He implies here that British electronic media coverage can often be wildly exaggerated (1). They were suggesting that the rain had been a 'biblical deluge' (comparing the rain to Noah's flood) (1) when in fact only a tiny number of homes had been seriously affected. (1)

3 **Extract from Christopher Nicol, *Eric Linklater's 'Private Angelo' and 'The Dark of Summer'*, ASLS, Glasgow 2012**

   a After the war (1), the book reviewers (1) started to focus more and more on newer writers. (1)

   b He implies that if a writer produces a substantial body of work, he is likely to be remembered after his death (1). 'His place in the canon of Scottish literature' he thinks might be 'assured' (1), suggesting his belief that lasting fame and productivity are somehow connected. (1)

ANALYSIS QUESTIONS, PAGES 13–23

WORD CHOICE

Remember that we are focusing here on how to approach word-choice questions. In the exam, however, you might interpret 'uses language' in a way that brings up discussion of more than word choice.

Extract from James Harkin, 'Living in Cyburbia', in the *Telegraph*, 29 January 2011

1 'conversion' suggests that the professor started with one opinion and then changed to another one (2), like one person changing from one religion to another.

   'digital utopian' suggests that she originally believed the digital age was wonderful, while 'digital realist' suggests she has now become more pragmatic in how she judges the age, seeing it with less rosy-tinted glasses. (2)

2 'nurturing friendships' contrasts with 'fire off [Facebook] messages'. By nurturing we are taking close care of something, but firing off suggests we are acting without real care or even attention. (2)

   'real human relationships' contrasts with 'relentless cycle' of 'cursory messages'. The former suggests thoughtful attention to and communication with people; the latter suggests a constant flow of highly superficial communications. Together they suggest we are turning from real friendship to a far less supportive replacement. (2)

IMAGERY

Extract from Jan Morris, *Venice*, Faber and Faber, London, 1993

Remember that in these exercises we are concentrating on imagery **and** word choice as we develop our skills. In the exam, the word 'language' in the question offers you the opportunity to discuss more than simply imagery and word choice. But, for the moment, let's keep things simple and revise what we have been learning about these two topics. As you will see, separating word choice and imagery can sometimes be a complex challenge.

1 'luscious': this word choice is particularly effective in conveying the texture of the Basin's water at night since it is usually associated with fruit, not water, and the reader is reminded of the thick juiciness of the mentioned plum-juice, suggesting also by its onomatopoeia the dense smoothness of the water. (2)

   'as a great lake of plum-juice': this simile is effective both in suggesting the dark, purplish colour of the water and suggesting a texture that seems much thicker than might be expected of water. It is also startling in suggesting that this plum- juice is covering an area far beyond what we might normally expect such a liquid to cover. (2)

2 'slowly sinking': this word choice makes the Doge's Palace appear like a damaged ocean-going vessel, which is gradually going down to the bottom of the sea, rather than the solid building that it is. (2)

contd

'like a pastry pavilion': this simile is effective in making the Palace sound precarious since, just as pastry is a delicate, vulnerable material that would disintegrate on contact with water, so, too, does the Palace appear similarly fragile and in equal danger of disintegrating because of its proximity to the water of the Basin. (2)

Extract from James Harkin, 'A whole new e-chapter' in the *Guardian*, 26 April 2011

1 'big beasts...struggle': this metaphor for the larger publishers effectively illustrates the way that they are dealing with their problems. Just as a big beast in the jungle would struggle to extricate itself from a trap, so, too, are the publishers thrashing about, trying to come up with a solution to their situation – and are having difficulty in so doing (2). On the other hand, 'a tiny east London publisher' 'knocks out' attractive solutions to the publishing crisis. The word choice of 'tiny' underlines that success is not dependent on size, for 'knocks out' suggests the careless ease with which these small publishers can effortlessly come up with solutions. (2)

2 a Nowadays, we are reluctant to be 'consuming random gobbets' of electronic information as we once did. This eating metaphor suggests that we once found satisfaction in devouring the bits and pieces offered by shorter programmes (2) but now we are 'hungry for' longer programmes 'to get our teeth into'. By extending this use of the eating image, the writer emphasises the contrast between unsatisfying past viewing and more satisfying current viewing habits. (2)

2 b Casual viewing habits he refers to as 'snacking on bite-sized nuggets', suggesting in this eating metaphor a contrast to a 'richer diet' of television we expect when we get home in the evening (2). Just as a snack will satisfy a passing, casual hunger, so too will a shorter programme satisfy at work, but when we get home we expect something more substantial to eat – and watch. (2)

3 He sees television as 'liberating' itself from the old programme formats and 'stretching [out]', like some confined creature finding a new freedom of movement (2). This metaphor of liberation suggests he takes an encouraging attitude to the new developments in television schedules. (2)

SENTENCE STRUCTURE/PUNCTUATION

Extract from George R. R. Martin, *A Clash of Kings*, Voyager, 1999

There are various possibilities here. Any two will be enough to achieve 4 marks.

- The **parallel structure** of verb + 'no' + noun ('take no wife, hold no lands, father no children') emphasises in its **repetition** the man's strength of purpose to forego any of these pleasures until he has done his duty. (2)

- The **parallel structure** of verb + 'no' + noun in 'wear no crowns' and 'win no glory' emphasises in its **repetition** the speaker's refusal to accept rewards until his duty is fulfilled.

- The **parallel structure** of 'I am the + noun + prepositional phrase' ('I am the sword in the darkness. I am the watcher on the walls') emphasises in its **repetition** the speaker's determination to be vigilant and his willingness to fight to live up to his oath. (2)

- The speaker extends the previous **parallel structure** to: 'I am the + noun + that + verb phrase' ('I am the fire that burns against the cold'). By using this structure four times, the writer emphasises in his **repetition** the speaker's determination to do his duty on many fronts and live fully up to his oath. (2)

- You might also wish to regard this paragraph as a series of **lists** underlining the speaker's determination to work tirelessly in many areas to uphold his oath. You would need to quote items from your selected list to achieve your full mark. (2)

Extract where the writer describes her childhood neighbourhood

1 a The use of the **colon** introduces an upcoming **list** of the seemingly endless nature of the street in the child's eyes: 'row of dowdy shops', 'series of tall tenements', 'windowless walls' which just went on and on. The fact that this description also occupies a **long sentence** further emphasises the way the street seemed to go on and on forever in the child's mind.

   b By using **repetition of** certain negative phrases in **parallel structures**, the writer suggests the unchanging nature of the street: 'never seemed to be bought', 'never seemed to lift', 'never seemed to disperse'. (3)

2 The park's significance in the child's mind is given emphasis by the use of the **short sentence** 'But then there was the park.' Coming as it does immediately **after a long sentence**, its effect is further intensified. (2)

3 By using two **rhetorical questions** 'Why is it that ...?' and 'How is it that ...?', the writer intends by this device to win readers to her point of view (2). This effect is further intensified by the use of **parallel structures** 'Why/How + is it that?' (2)

Extract about Harry being followed at night

1 By opening the passage with a series of three **short sentences**, the writer creates an atmosphere of tension (2). The tension is later continued with other **minor sentences** 'Tap, tap', 'No' and 'No answer' which intensify the tense effect. (2)

2 Harry appears through the writer's use of language to be a logical kind of person. He asks himself **questions** 'Was it footsteps ...?' and 'So why couldn't he ...?' and then analyses the **answers** carefully: 'No. It was more like a stick. Yes, a walking stick.' The brisk **short sentences** convey the straightforward, rational nature of the boy (2). His **exclamations** 'Hey, you! Show yourself!' reveal he is capable of strong responses and is not fearful in this tense situation. (2)

contd

ANSWERS

TONE

TTDATA activity

Tone	Possible markers
1. Emotive	Repetition of emotive phrases: 'a generous America, ... a compassionate America, ... a tolerant America'. Repetition of emotion-rousing situations: 'to the dreams of an immigrant's daughter', 'to the young boy on the south side ...'. Ends on a list of emotionally charged ambitions, building to a climax on the word 'president'.
2. Ironic	Writer calls it 'finest' summer yet describes a series of disasters: 'basement flooded', 'caught pneumonia', 'unemployed'. He is describing the very opposite of what he says: 'a great season all round' and 'One of the very best'.
3. Persuasive	'For generations', 'the test of time', 'finest in its class', 'touchstone of excellence', 'beacon of perfection', 'only the best will do'.
4. Mixes colloquial with persuasive	Colloquial markers: free use of pronouns 'I' and 'you'. Informal commands: 'Turn ...', 'Go ...', Read ...'. Chatty expressions: 'winging its way', 'lickety-split'. Short sentences: 'How so?' Rhetorical questions: 'Who wouldn't want ...?' Persuasive markers: 'parents proud', 'sweet smell of success', 'seal of approval'.
5. Factual/ matter-of fact	Series of statements: 'is 100,000 higher than ...' '1.5 million more adults are playing sport'. Use of statistics: '15.5 million'. Neutral, unemotional language: 'The number of people', 'bid for the Olympics'. Note also the absence of personal pronouns, rhetorical questions, emotive phrases and abbreviations.

MARKING GUIDELINES FOR ELIZABETH GILBERT: *SUCCESS, FAILURE AND THE DRIVE TO KEEP CREATING*

1 To inform listeners about her discovery of where happiness lies in life as she reports factually on life experiences she has undergone.
OR
To persuade/reassure listeners that happiness is possible as she uses repetition and targeted climax towards the end to emphasise that contentment comes by returning constantly to what it is you love best.

2 Those with a specific interest in the career of a well-known authoress as she details some surprising personal information about the follow-up to her greatest publishing success.

Those interested generally in discovering personal wellbeing/happiness as she includes practical advice on how to survive the ups and downs of life to which we are all subject.

3 It is effective as an introduction to this talk since it establishes the kind of character Gilbert is: she can laugh at herself, thus displaying a balanced view of life. This is important, as she is proposing later how we can find happiness. Her use of a humorous anecdote told in colloquial terms: 'Honey, I gotta aks you ...' and her reference to 'tough-talking ... broads' positions the tone of the talk.

4 'Going home' did not mean returning to her family's farm but rather to an activity – writing – that she felt was her real home, since she loved it more than she loved anything else in life, even herself.

5 a She uses repetition of the word 'love' when applied to writing five times in close proximity to each other. b For her, writing is not an activity but is her 'home'. c She uses a long, complex sentence with two 'which' clauses to emphasise with the greatest care the particular nature/ the intensity of her love for writing.

6 Central to Gilbert's life was the activity of creating/ writing. Failure, which she felt when a waitress, and success, which she experienced after the publication of her bestseller, were merely disruptive distractions from her core activity of writing. Success and failure were both equally irrelevant; only writing mattered.

7 Repetition of phrase 'it might be'. The effect is to emphasise the multiple possibilities that people have to find happiness. Repetition of 'another' (referring to future writing projects). The effect is to underline the never-ending nature of her commitment to writing, no matter the success or failure of individual books. Repetition of 'again' to emphasise the need to keep returning to whatever it is that makes you happy, no matter what the distraction.

'Right?': A very brief rhetorical question whose effect is to seek the audience's agreement/approval.

'many of them will fail' ... 'some of them might succeed': Parallel structures emphasise the possibly contrasting fates of the books which Gilbert accepts without question.

8 a The link is the importance of finding your home. She has explained in great detail where her home is and its importance to her ultimate happiness. Her advice to the audience is to seek out **their** home and stay with it to find the happiness Gilbert has found through writing.

b All through the talk, with her informal tone ('get my ass back to work') and her use of 'you' in addressing her audience constantly, she has been creating a warm bond with her listeners. It is an effective way to end the talk since, in wishing them a 'home' for themselves, it is her parting good wish to them to find happiness and fulfilment.

INDEX